D0311981

Naming Day Sept · 6th 1998

To fred
"Your a Star" ✡

All or love +
Kisses

Auntie Suzie, Uncle Peter
Maxwell +
Benedict

∞ ∞ ∞ ∞ ∞

The
ILLUSTRATED
Book of
MYTHS

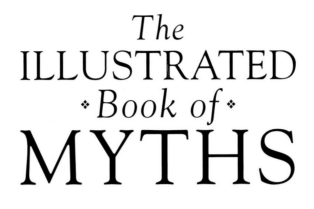

*Tezcatlipoca shows Quetzalcoatl his new, human
face and body in a smoking mirror, page 140*

The
ILLUSTRATED
❖ *Book of* ❖
MYTHS

Tales & Legends of the World

Retold by
NEIL PHILIP

Illustrated by
NILESH MISTRY

DORLING KINDERSLEY

London • New York • Stuttgart

A DORLING KINDERSLEY BOOK

❖

Senior Art Editor
Jacquie Gulliver

Research
Robert Graham

Senior Editors
Alastair Dougall
Emma Johnson

Production
Josie Alabaster
Louise Barratt

Designers
Lester Cheeseman
Sheilagh Noble

Managing Art Editor
Peter Bailey

Managing Editor
Helen Parker

Picture Research
Sharon Southren

Consultant
Sandra Dudley, Jesus College, Oxford

❖

for
BRIAN HINTON

First published in Great Britain in 1995
by Dorling Kindersley Limited, 9 Henrietta Street, London WC2E 8PS

Reprinted 1995

A CIP catalogue record for this book is available from the British Library

ISBN 0 7513 53175

Reproduced by Classic Scan, Singapore
Printed and bound in Spain by Artes Graficas
D.L.TO:1253-1995

CONTENTS

The Emperor of Heaven looks down on the poor people struggling to survive on earth and decides to help them, page 52

The abandoned babes Romulus and Remus are looked after by a she-wolf, page 138

*The oracle of Apollo,
who tells mortals
of things to come,
page 96*

FERTILITY AND CULTIVATION

*Pandora releases evils
into the world, page 60*

GODS AND MORTALS

*The god Thor has
a drinking contest
with the giants,
page 122*

Thor tries to lift the giants' cat, page 123

GODS AND ANIMALS

Enkidu and Gilgamesh grapple with the Bull of Heaven, page 45

VISIONS OF THE END

GODS AND PANTHEONS

A bee is sent to sting the angry weather god Telepinu into seeing sense, page 95

The rampaging Cretan bull, which Heracles captured as his seventh Labour, page 132

The funeral ship of Balder, Odin's son, page 163

INTRODUCTION

MYTHS ARE STORIES of the gods and of god-like heroes. They tell of beginnings and ends, creation and destruction, life and death. They explain the how and the why of life.

The word "myth" comes from the Greek *muthos* meaning a fable or a word. The Greek myths about the gods of Olympus are a major source for Western art and literature, providing a treasure-trove of stories and images that artists and writers even today – long after belief in the Greek gods has vanished – can make fresh, new, and meaningful.

But, of course, the Greek myths are only a part of world mythology. Wherever people have lived together, they have told stories about how the world came to be made, how people and animals came to live in it, and the characters and actions of the god or gods they worshipped.

A nature-spirit mask of the Inuit people

When a myth comes into existence, it is believed in a people's heart and soul. Because of this, myths are more than just stories: every myth is a shaft of human truth.

Myths and their associated rituals have often been seen as precious secrets. Even today we do not fully know what happened at the "mysteries" of Eleusis, the ancient Greek fertility cult. The cult centred on the myth of the corn goddess Demeter and her daughter Persephone, but no-one ever dared reveal its secret rites.

The Medicine Rite of the Winnebago Sioux was equally secret. It warned: "Never tell anyone about this Rite. Keep it absolutely secret. If you disclose it the world will come to an end. We will all die . . ." By the time a member of the tribe, Jasper Blowsnake, revealed the secrets in 1908, the ancient world of the Winnebago had come to an end.

Thor, Norse god of thunder, strikes the sleeping giant Skrymir with his hammer

Aztec deity Quetzalcoatl, the plumed serpent god, with his dog-shaped twin, Xolotl

One person's myth is another's religious belief; one person's truth, another's fiction. Paul Radin, to whom Jasper Blowsnake told the secret of the Winnebago Medicine Rite, quoted the words of an Inuit leader named Anarulunguaq, who, when standing on the roof of a New York skyscraper, declared: "I see things more than my mind can grasp; and the only way to save oneself from madness is to suppose that we have all died suddenly before we knew, and that this is part of another life."

❖

Standing on the brink of this book, looking out over the myths of mankind, we too may feel lost. How can we begin to understand these stories, that meant so much to the people who told them and lived by them?

The best place to begin is at the beginning. All mythologies start by telling of the creation of the world. The Greeks, the Vikings, the Egyptians, the Chinese, the Japanese, all the peoples of Africa, and all the 500 nations of the Native Americans, each had their own version

or versions of the creation. And when you begin to compare all these stories, a fascinating pattern begins to emerge.

Myths are the dreams of mankind. Like dreams, they are at once utterly strange and hauntingly familiar. The Aboriginal people of Australia, for whom myths are the true reality, call the time in which the world was created – and the ancestors shaped the land, created human beings and established their customs – the Dreamtime. However the Dreamtime is not an event in the long-distant past; it is an eternal present, part of the "dreaming", which forms a living tie between the people, the eternal ancestors, and the land. For Aboriginals, this living tie is illustrated by the "song lines", the paths that trace the Dreamtime wanderings of the eternal ancestors.

All these song lines converge at the most sacred place of all to the Aboriginals, Uluru, formerly known to white Australians as Ayers Rock. When an Aboriginal tells, enacts, or depicts the song lines, he or she actually enters the dreaming.

Persephone, daughter of the Greek goddess Demeter, pines in the Underworld

Outsiders can scarcely hope to have the same, intense experience of a myth that enables an insider to savour its full and true meaning. There will always be things we are unable to understand or appreciate, or which have been distorted in translation or retelling. But as with poetry, myths repel those who want to explain them away, and invite in those willing to listen and learn. As the ancient Greek writer Aristotle said: "The friend of wisdom is also a friend of myth."

Myths couch their wisdom, their inner meaning and mystery, in the form of stories. People everywhere love to tell and to hear stories, and that is why the myths came into being, and how they survived, and how they grew and changed. Teller and listener, when sharing a myth, are sharing a secret that will enrich them both. The poet W. H. Auden's translation of the Norse mythological poem "The Words of the High One" ends:

"Hail to the speaker, hail to the knower,
Joy to him who has understood,
Delight to those who have listened."

Joy, understanding, and delight; speech, listening, and knowledge. These are the essentials of a myth.

Norse mythology is recorded in poems that date back to when the Vikings worshipped the Norse gods, and also in prose versions written after the Vikings had converted to Christianity. At the changeover period, pagan and Christian stories often converged. Thus one side of a cross in Gosforth churchyard, Cumbria, England, shows scenes from Ragnarok, the Norse gods' final battle, and the other the crucifixion of Jesus. The Vikings were a warlike people, and when they developed their own myths from those of more peaceful Germanic tribes, they shifted the emphasis from agriculture to battle.

THE WESTERN HEMISPHERE

Kumush, the Old Man of the Ancients in the myths of the Maidu

NORTH AMERICA

Quetzalcoatl, creator god of the Aztecs

NATIVE AMERICAN
These myths have grown up from the hundreds of indigenous cultures that have evolved in North America.

AZTEC
This empire lasted from c.1200 BC to AD 1519, when it was crushed by Spanish invaders. This date had been accurately prophesied by Aztec myth.

❖ EUROPE
The conversion to Christianity of the Roman Emperor Constantine in AD 312 signalled the end for the mythologies of Greece and Rome as living religions, and also for Celtic and Germanic deities. In Scandinavia, however, the pagan Norse gods were worshipped until the 12th century.

❖ AFRICA
Many indigenous African gods and myths co-exist with Christianity and Islam. Some myths, transported to the New World by slaves, mutated into the Voodoo religion, based in Haiti.

❖ AMERICA
The Aztec and the Inca empires were destroyed by European invaders, and many of their myths were lost. The cost of recording the beautiful mythologies of native American tribes has been the destruction of their traditional culture.

The Norse giant Hugi outruns the mortal Thialfi

NORSE
The Norse myths were not set down until the 13th century, after Scandinavia had converted to Christianity.

Merlin, the enchanter of Celtic myth

EUROPE

GREEK
From c.800 BC to 330 BC, belief in the Greek gods was at its peak. Many deities were adopted, under different names, by the Roman Empire.

The oracle of Apollo, Greek god of the sun

CELTIC
From c.750 BC to AD 100, Celts occupied northern Europe. Their myths were set down by Roman historians and Christian priests, and greatly added to in the Middle Ages.

Osiris, Egyptian fertility god, and Set, god of evil

Papa Ghede, Voodoo god of death

EGYPTIAN
The ancient Egyptian religion was at its height between c.3100 BC, when the kingdom was united, to about 30 BC.

AFRICA

A doll, made by Kwaku-Ananse the spider, to catch Mmoatia, the spirit

HAITIAN
The myths of Voodoo, the popular religion of Haiti are a blend of West African beliefs and Catholicism.

SOUTH AMERICA

AFRICAN
Many native African religions survive today, occasionally spreading to other parts of the world, such as Haiti.

THE EASTERN HEMISPHERE

ASIA

The dog – fated to serve people by Ulgan, the Siberian creator god

SIBERIAN
Myths may date back over 10,000 years to the last Ice Age, when nomadic tribes came to inhabit the Steppes.

Anu, the Sumerian sky god

The dragon and the unicorn are sacred animals in Chinese myth

The sandals of Ainu hero Aioina turn into squirrels

SUMERIAN
These myths date from at least 3500 BC. Elements from Sumerian mythology were absorbed into Christian traditions.

CHINESE
Folk myths and traditions date back to c. 2000 BC. Some were absorbed into the Taoist religion, which developed about AD 200. With Confucianism and Buddhism, Taoism is one of the main Chinese religions.

JAPANESE
The Shinto religion, which dates back to the 8th century and beyond to ancient traditions, has a rich mythology. The myths of the Ainu, Japan's first inhabitants, also survive.

Ganesha, Hindu god of wisdom

INDIAN
Hinduism, the dominant religion of India, dates back to at least 1200 BC, the date of the first Hindu texts, called the Vedas.

Bamapama, an Aboriginal trickster god

ABORIGINAL
Myths of the Dreamtime have evolved over 40,000 years, ever since the first people arrived in Australia from Asia.

AUSTRALASIA

A sea beast created *from the fingers of Sedna, the Inuit goddess of the sea*

INUIT
Belief in the nature spirits of Inuit mythology is alive. The Inuit have lived in the Arctic circle for over 10,000 years.

OCEANIC
Before the islanders of the South Pacific became Christians during the 19th century, they worshipped many different gods. Polynesia possessed the most organized mythology.

The sun, caught by Polynesian hero Maui

OCEANIA

❖ AUSTRALASIA AND OCEANIA
For the Australian Aboriginals, everything in the world is sacred because of its association with the Dreamtime ancestors. This makes their mythology absolutely central to their existence. In Polynesian mythology too, life, belief, and the land are very closely linked.

❖ ASIA
These simple – though profound and wise – mythologies contrast with the complex Hindu mythology of India, which reflects its long smelting in the cultural melting pot of the Indian sub-continent. Similarly, the mythologies of China and Japan have developed in the light of sophisticated philosophies. Nevertheless, every mythology, like every religion, shares the same basic concern with the nature of the world, and the meaning of life and death.

All mythologies reflect the culture they serve. A farming people, such as the Chinese or the ancient Egyptians, especially venerated gods of agriculture and fertility. By contrast, the myths of Australian Aboriginals, who were hunter-gatherers not farmers, contain the sacred information of how to survive in Australia's vast, bare hinterland.

❖

The stories in this book are just a fraction of the tales that make up world mythology, and some regions are better represented than others. The stories that have been written down are also just a fraction of those that have, throughout history, expressed the fears, hopes and longings of humanity. Some myths have vanished almost without trace; others exist only as obscure fragments.

So we must be thankful to those who have recorded ancient myths for our delight and understanding. One such was Sandoval, Hastin Tlo'tsi hee, who told anthropologist Aileen O'Bryan the creation myth of the Navajo in November 1928. "I sit as on a mountaintop and I look into the future," he said. "I see my people and your people living together. In time to come, my people will have forgotten their early way of life unless they learn it from white man's books. So you must write down what I tell you; and have it made into a book that coming generations may know the truth."

Hail to the speaker, hail to the knower!

CREATION MYTHS

How did the world begin? How were people created, and why? And, when once we had been given life, why were we cursed with death? These are the first questions that the mythologies of the world attempt to answer.

Different cultures have found different solutions to these fundamental problems, but the stories in which those solutions are presented often follow a similar pattern. In the beginning, the world is in chaos, or covered in ice, or swamped with water.

A creator god comes and sets to work, separating the earth from the heavens, the sea from the land, and shaping the landscape. Then the creator peoples the earth, making human beings from drops of sweat, from plants and animals, from mud – or even from his own fleas. And then the real work starts.

Adapa breaks the South Wind's wing, and so incurs the wrath of Anu the sky god in The Food of Life – *a story that tells why mortals are "creatures of time"*

FIRST THINGS

AT THE DAWN OF TIME, Re gave birth to himself. Feeling that he was alone, Re spat, and from his spittle were born Shu, the air, and Tefnut, moisture. From the union of Shu and Tefnut came Geb, the earth god, and Nut, the sky goddess.

From Re's tears came the first human beings. He knitted together the mountains, he made mankind and the beasts, the heavens and the earth.

Each morning he rises and sails in his boat, Sektet, across the sky. At night, Nut swallows him, and in the morning she gives birth to him once more.

Re

Shu

Tefnut

Nut

Geb

From his spittle, Re creates the universe

THE CREATOR
Re (or Ra), the sun god, was the most important god of the New Kingdom period (1560-1070 BC) in ancient Egypt. Sometimes he was identified with Amun-Re, known as the "hidden" god because of his mysterious nature. Re was also believed to be the creator of the universe.

The serpent Apep is his foe, born from the spittle of the Great Mother, Neith. Re spends each night in combat with Apep, the chaos serpent.

Nut swallows Re in his boat

Some believe that one day, Apep may succeed in devouring Re, and then the world will end. Others say that Re will grow so old and tired that he will forget who he is. All that he has created will come to nothing.

And then, perhaps, Re will give birth to himself again.

Each night Re struggles with the serpent Apep

The Cat Goddess, page 146 ➤

THE SWEAT OF HIS BROW

God wakes up from a long sleep

IN THE BEGINNING THERE was nothing but God, and God slept and dreamed. For many ages, God dreamed. But at last he awoke.

Having roused himself from sleep, God looked around him, and every glance became a star. God was amazed. He began to travel, to see the universe he had created. He travelled and travelled, but wherever he went there was neither end nor limit.

At last he arrived on earth. He was weary and sweat clung to his brow. A drop fell to the ground, and became alive; thus the first man was made. He is God's kin, but he was not created for pleasure. He was produced from sweat and, from the beginning, he was doomed to a life of toil.

God travels the universe until he is weary and covered in sweat

A drop of sweat falls from God's brow and becomes the first man

OUT OF THE ICE

NORSE WARRIOR
This 12th-century
Swedish wall-hanging
of a warrior or king is
often thought to be of
Odin, the chief god of
Norse mythology. It is
said that Odin knew
everything that went
on in the world.

❖

THE FROST GIANTS
All of the frost giants
were descended from
the first giant, Ymir.
They were constantly
at war with the gods, of
whom they were jealous.
Often they tried to steal
the gods' treasures or
gain power over them.

ODIN IS THE ALL-FATHER. He is the oldest and most powerful of the Norse gods. Through the ages he has ruled all things. He created heaven and earth, and he made man and gave him a soul. But even the All-Father was not the very first. Listen!

In the beginning, there was no earth, no sea, no sky. Only the emptiness of Ginnungagap, waiting to be filled. In the south, the fiery realm of Muspell came into being, and in the north, the icy

As the ice melts, it shapes itself into the giant Ymir

realm of Niflheim. Fire and ice played across the emptiness. And in the centre of nothingness the air grew mild. Where the warm air from Muspell met the cool air from Niflheim, the ice began to thaw. As it dripped, it shaped itself into the form of a giant. His name was Ymir, and he was evil.

As Ymir slept, he began to sweat. There grew beneath his left arm a male and a female, and from his legs another male was created. These were the first frost giants, all descended from Ymir.

Then the ice-melt formed a cow, named Audhumla. Four rivers of milk flowed from her teats and fed Ymir. Audhumla nourished herself by licking the ice. She licked the salty blocks of ice and by the end of the first day she had uncovered the hair of a head. By the end of the second day the whole head was exposed, and by the end of the third day there was a complete man. His name was Buri and he was strong and handsome. Buri had a son named Bor, who married Bestla, the daughter of one of the frost giants. Bor and Bestla had three sons: Odin, Vili, and Ve.

The cow Audhumla licks the salty ice until she uncovers the head of a man

LAND OF FIRE

It is not hard to see where the inspiration for the fiery realm of Muspell came from. Iceland is a country of volcanoes and bubbling geysers, as well as icy glaciers. The fountain of Strokkur, shown above, is Iceland's most impressive geyser. The tranquil surface of the pool is suddenly broken as the geyser swells, creating a dome that bursts explosively. This dramatic eruption occurs roughly every nine minutes.

From the sweat beneath Ymir's left arm, a male and a female frost giant grow; from his legs, a male giant emerges

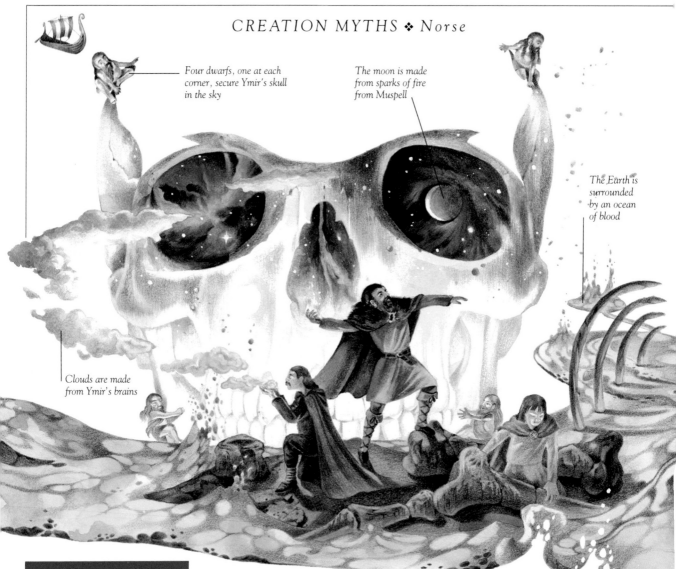

Four dwarfs, one at each corner, secure Ymir's skull in the sky

The moon is made from sparks of fire from Muspell

The Earth is surrounded by an ocean of blood

Clouds are made from Ymir's brains

Odin and his brothers make the earth from Ymir's flesh, and rocks and stones from his teeth and bones

ROCKY GIANTS
Weathered by wind, water and ice, rocks like this one in Sweden look like giant mythological figures.

Odin and his brothers hated the brutal frost giant Ymir, and they slew him. So much blood flowed from the slaughtered giant that it drowned all the frost giants save Bergelmir and his wife, who escaped in a boat made from a hollowed tree trunk.

From Ymir's flesh, Odin and his brothers made the earth, and from his shattered bones and teeth, they made the rocks and stones. From Ymir's blood, they made the rivers and lakes, and they circled the earth with an ocean of blood.

Ymir's skull they set in the sky, secured at four points by the four dwarfs named East, West, North, and South. They flung sparks of fire from Muspell high into the sky to make the sun, the moon, and the stars. From Ymir's brains, they shaped the clouds.

The earth was made in the form of a circle, and around the edge of it lay the great sea. Odin and his brothers gave Utgard to the giants as their citadel. And for themselves they established the kingdom of Asgard, protecting it from the giants with fortifications made from Ymir's eyebrows.

As they walked along the shore of the great sea, Odin and his brothers came across two logs. Odin gave them breath and life; Vili gave them brains and feelings; and Ve gave them hearing and sight. These were the first man, Ask, and the first woman, Embla, and Midgard was their home. From them, all the families of mankind are descended.

Below Midgard is the icy realm of death, Niflheim. Above it is the realm of the gods, Asgard, where Odin sits on his throne and watches over all the worlds. Asgard and Midgard are linked by the rainbow bridge, Bifrost.

At the centre of all the realms is the great ash tree, Yggdrasil, whose branches shade the world, and whose roots support it.

The land of Midgard is protected by Ymir's eyebrows

❖

BIFROST
The way into Asgard, home of the Norse gods, was over a fiery rainbow bridge called Bifrost. Only the gods could cross this bridge, which was intended to keep mortals and giants out of Asgard. Bifrost was guarded by the god Heimdall.

❖

ASK AND EMBLA
In Norse myth the first people were Ask and Embla. They were made by the gods from two logs, one thought to be an ash (Ask).

Ask

Embla

Odin and his brothers create the first man and woman from two logs on the shore

The Tree of Life, page 62 ➤

THE COSMIC EGG

YOUNG MOUNTAINS
The sharp limestone peaks of this landscape in southeastern China have been created comparatively recently by the erosive power of wind and water. They form a fitting backdrop to this story, which describes a world where humans are just insignificant fleas compared to the majesty of nature.

❖

YIN AND YANG
In ancient Chinese philosophy, all things are believed to combine the two opposites, Yin and Yang. Yin is negative, cold, dark, heavy, and feminine, while Yang is positive, light, bright, warm, and masculine. The symbol for Yin and Yang is a diagram of an egg divided into yolk and white, dark and light – Yin and Yang.

AT THE BEGINNING of time, all was chaos, and this chaos was shaped like a hen's egg. Inside the egg were Yin and Yang, the two opposing forces of which the universe is made. Yin and Yang are darkness and light, female and male, cold and hot, wet and dry.

One day, the warring energies inside this egg rent it apart. The heavier elements sank, to form the earth, and the lighter ones floated, to form the sky. And between the earth and the sky was P'an-ku, the first being. Every day for eighteen thousand years, the earth and the sky separated a little further, and every day P'an-ku grew at the same rate, so that he always filled the space between them.

*P'an-ku, the first being, bursts out of the cosmic egg
and keeps apart Yin and Yang, earth and sky*

P'an-ku's body was covered with thick hair, and he had two horns thrusting from his forehead and two tusks from his upper jaw. When he was happy, the weather was fine, but if he grew troubled or angry, it rained or a storm blew up.

People tell two different stories about the great P'an-ku. Some say that, exhausted by the labour of keeping earth and sky apart while the world took shape, he died. His body split asunder, so that his head became the mountain of the north, his stomach the mountain of the centre, his left arm the mountain of the east, his right arm the mountain of the west, and his feet the mountain of the south. His eyes became the sun and moon, his flesh the land, his hair the trees and plants, and his tears the rivers and seas. His breath became the wind, and his voice the thunder and lightning.

When he dies, P'an-ku's eyes become the sun and moon

P'an-ku's fleas became mankind.

However, others say that P'an-ku, in company with the first tortoise, the first phoenix, the first dragon, and the first unicorn, wrought the universe into shape with his hammer and chisel. He ruled mankind in the first epoch of history. Every day he instructed them from his high throne, until they knew all about the sun and the moon and the stars above, and the four seas below. Listening to him, people lost their tiredness.

One morning, however, when the great P'an-ku had passed on all his wisdom to mankind, he disappeared and was never

The first people, all descended from P'an-ku's fleas, stand before his throne – but P'an-ku has vanished

SPECIAL ANIMALS
In one of the stories about P'an-ku, he goes about the world accompanied by four imaginary animals that were highly symbolic to the ancient Chinese: a dragon, the chief of all scaly creatures; a tortoise, the chief of all creatures with shells; the phoenix, the most important of feathered creatures; and the unicorn, chief of all animals with hair.

IMPERIAL DRAGON
This 14th-century imperial seal features a five-toed dragon, the symbol of the Emperor of China. Dragons represented wisdom, strength and goodness, and the life-giving power of water.

The Phoenix, page 151 ▶

THE FLOATING WORLD

JAPANESE WAGTAIL
This pied wagtail ranges widely over Asia and is popular in Japanese as well as Ainu myth. A wagtail made the Shinto gods Izanami and Izanagi fall in love. Wagtail bones and feathers are still used as love charms.

IN THE BEGINNING, the world was nothing but a slushy quagmire. The water and the earth were all mixed up and there was nothing but a great swamp. Nothing could live there. But in the six skies above and in the six worlds below dwelt gods, demons, and animals.

In the fog skies and hanging skies of the lower heavens, demons lived. In the star-bearing skies and the high skies of the clouds lived the lesser gods. In the skies of the most high lived Kamui, the creator god, and his servants. His realm was surrounded by a mighty metal wall and the only entrance was through a great iron gate.

Kamui made this world as a vast round ocean, resting on the backbone of an enormous trout. This fish sucks in the ocean and spits it out again to make the tides; when it moves it causes earthquakes.

One day, Kamui looked down on the watery world and decided to make something of it. He sent down a water wagtail to do the work. When the poor bird arrived and saw what a mess everything was

When the enormous trout spits, it creates the ocean tides

in, it was at its wits' end to know what to do. However, by fluttering over the waters with its wings and by trampling the mud with its feet and beating it with its tail, the wagtail at last created patches of dry land. In this way islands were raised to float upon the ocean in this, the floating world. Even today, the faithful wagtail is still carrying on its work, still beating the ground with its tail.

When Kamui created the world, the devil tried to thwart him. One morning, the devil got up and lay in wait with his mouth gaping wide to swallow the sun. But Kamui sent a crow to fly down the devil's throat and make him choke and cough. That is why the crow is such a bold bird. Because a crow once saved the world, all crows think they can act as they like, even stealing people's food.

When the animals who lived up in the heavens saw how beautiful the world was, they begged Kamui to let them come and live here, and he did. But Kamui also made many other creatures especially for this world.

The wagtail makes islands by fluttering its wings, trampling with its feet and beating its tail

ISLAND PEOPLE
The Shiretoko peninsula is a long finger of land that reaches out into the Sea of Okhotsk from a "floating world" – the northern Japanese island of Hokkaido. The island is still home to the people who tell this story, the Ainu, Japan's first ever inhabitants.

The first people, the Ainu, had bodies of earth, hair of chickweed, and spines made from sticks of willow. That is why when we grow old, our backs become bent.

Kamui sent Aioina, the divine man, down from heaven to teach the Ainu how to hunt and to cook. When Aioina returned to heaven after living among people and teaching them many things, the gods all held their noses, crying, "What a terrible smell of human being there is!"

They sniffed and sniffed to find out where the stink was coming from. At last they traced the smell to Aioina's clothes. The gods sent him back to earth and refused to let him back into heaven until he left all his clothes behind. Down in the floating world, Aioina's cast-off sandals turned into the first squirrels.

Aioina's old sandals turn into the world's first squirrels

IZANAMI AND IZANAGI

I N THE BEGINNING, HEAVEN and earth were not divided. Then, from the ocean of chaos, arose a reed, and that was the eternal land ruler, Kunitokotatchi.

Then came the female god, Izanami, and the male, Izanagi. They stood on the floating bridge of heaven and stirred the ocean with a jewelled spear until it curdled, and so created the first island, Onokoro. They built a house on this island, with a central stone pillar that is the backbone of the world. Izanami walked one way around the pillar, and Izanagi walked the other. When they met face to face, they united in marriage.

Their first child was named Hiruko, but he did not thrive, so when he was three, they placed him in a reed boat and set him adrift; he became Ebisu, god of fishermen.

Then Izanami gave birth to the eight islands of Japan.

And finally Izanami began to give birth to the gods who would fashion and rule the world – gods of the sea and gods of the land, gods of wind and rain. But when Izanami gave birth to the god of fire, she was so badly burned that she died.

Izanagi was furious with the fire god and cut him into three pieces. Then he set out to search for Izanami. He went right down into the Land of Gloom looking for her. He called her, saying, "Come back, my love. The lands we are making are not yet finished!"

She came to him, saying, "You are too late. I have already eaten the food of this land. But I would like to return. Wait here for me, and I will ask permission from the spirits of the underworld. But do not try to look at me."

At length, Izanagi got tired of waiting, so he broke off a tooth from the comb he wore in his hair to use as a torch and followed her. When he found her, he saw that she was already rotting, and maggots were swarming over her body. She was giving birth to the eight gods of thunder.

Izanagi drew back, revolted. Izanami called after him, "Shame on you." She commanded the foul spirits of the underworld to slay him.

BRIDGE OF HEAVEN
This sandbar, covered with pines, runs right across Japan's Wakasa Bay. Its name, Amanohashidate, means "Bridge of Heaven", recalling the myth of Izanami and Izanagi.

Izanagi stirs the ocean with a spear to create the first island

While the spirits of the Land of Gloom devour bamboo shoots, Izanagi escapes

The spirits pursued Izanagi, but he managed to escape. He threw down his headdress and it turned into grapes, which the spirits stopped to eat. Then he threw down his comb, which turned into bamboo shoots, and once again the spirits stopped to eat.

By the time Izanagi reached the pass between the land of the dead and the land of the living, Izanami herself had nearly caught up with him. But Izanagi saw her coming and quickly blocked the pass with a huge boulder that it would take a thousand men to lift, so making a permanent barrier between life and death.

Standing on the other side of the boulder, Izanami shouted, "Every day I will kill a thousand people, and bring them to this land!"

❖

THE KOJIKI
The story of Izanagi and Izanami forms part of Shinto, Japan's oldest religion. Along with many other tales, this story was preserved by storytellers, who sang them at religious festivals. The stories were not written down until the 8th century, when the Empress Gemmyo had the Shinto legends collected in a book called *Kojiki* or "Record of Ancient Things".

To escape Izanami's fury, Izanagi blocks the pass to the Land of Gloom with a huge boulder

Izanagi replied, "Every day I will cause one thousand five hundred babies to be born."

Then Izanagi left Izanami to rule the Land of Gloom, and returned to the land of the living.

Izanagi came to a grove of orange trees on a plain covered with bush clover. There he bathed at the mouth of a clear stream and, as he washed the filth of the underworld from his face, more gods were born. He wiped his left eye, and created Amaterasu, goddess of the sun. He wiped his right eye, and created Tsuki-yomi, god of the moon. He wiped his nose, and created Susanowo, god of the tempest.

When Izanagi wipes his right eye after washing in a stream, he gives birth to the moon god, Tsuki-yomi

27

World Without Sun, page 84 ➤

THE DREAMTIME

BURNING WILDERNESS
The vast Simpson Desert
of central Australia is
one of the hottest places
in the world. But, to
Aboriginals, even this
forbidding landscape
has meaning, and
bears the traces of the
eternal ancestors.

❖

ALCHERA
The story of the
Dreamtime told here
belongs to the Aranda
Aboriginals of central
Australia. Their name
for the Dreamtime is
"Alchera". A huge
number of myths
associated with the
Dreamtime are told by
Aboriginal peoples.
These myths tell how
the landscape was
shaped and explain the
characteristics of
animals and birds. For
Aboriginals, the
Dreamtime becomes
part of the present when
its myths of creation are
relived by being acted
out in holy ceremonies.

IN THE BEGINNING the earth was a bare plain. All was dark.
There was no life and no death. The sun, the moon, and the
stars slept beneath the earth. All the eternal ancestors slept
there too, until at last they woke themselves out of their own
eternity and broke through to the surface.

When the eternal ancestors arose, they wandered the earth,
sometimes in animal form – as kangaroos, or emus, or lizards –
sometimes in human shape, sometimes part animal and
human, sometimes part human and plant.

Two such beings, self-created out of nothing, were the
Ungambikula. Wandering the world, they found half-made people.
They had been created out of animals and plants, but were shapeless
bundles, lying higgledy-piggledy, near where water holes and salt lakes
could be made. The people were all doubled over into balls, vague
and unfinished, without limbs or features.

*The eternal ancestors awake and wander the earth both
in human shape and in the forms of animals*

With their great stone knives, the Ungambikula carved out heads, bodies, legs and arms. They made the faces, and the hands and feet. At last the human beings were finished.

Every man and woman was transformed from a plant or an animal, and each person owes allegiance to the totem of the animal or the plant that they were made from – the plum tree, the grass seed, the large and small lizards, the parakeet, the rat.

TOOL OF LIFE
This stone knife (on right) was made by the Aranda Aboriginal people and found by a European expedition in 1906. The sheath is made of bark. In this story, the eternal ancestors, the Ungambikula, use similar knives to create humans in the Dreamtime.

One of the Ungambikula frees the limbs of a human being

SACRED PLACE
This Aboriginal painting is on Uluru (formerly known as Ayers Rock), a huge rock in central Australia. It is sacred to the Anangu people, who have lived in the region for over 20,000 years.

Their sacred work done, the ancestors went back to sleep. Some of them returned to underground homes, others became rocks and trees.

The trails the ancestors walked in the Dreamtime are holy trails. Everywhere the ancestors went, they left the sacred traces of their presence – a rock, a waterhole, a tree.

For the Dreamtime does not merely lie in the distant past, the Dreamtime is the eternal Now. Between heartbeat and heartbeat, the Dreamtime can come again.

Hunting the Sun, page 69 ➤

AN EARTHLY PARADISE

THE WISE LORD
An Assyrian king,
Shalmaneser II, pays
homage to the "Wise
Lord", Ahura Mazda
(left), in a relief from
the 8th century BC.
The winged disc in the
centre symbolizes Ahura
Mazda's power.

AT THE BEGINNING, the wise lord Ahura Mazda lived in the light; his twin, Angra Mainyu, known as Ahriman, lived in the dark. Between them there was only air.

Then Ahura Mazda created time, and the world began. He brought the sunlit days and set the stars to glitter in the sky; he made the moon wax and wane and yoked the swift lightning and loud thunder to the wind and clouds. He created the Good Mind, that works within man and all creation for the best; Love is his daughter.

Ahriman came to him, set about with demons, in anger and spite. Ahura Mazda welcomed his brother with words of peace, but Ahriman spurned him. So Ahura Mazda sent Ahriman back into the darkness whence he had come. He said, "Neither our thoughts, teachings, plans, beliefs, words, nor souls agree."

Ahura Mazda created the first man, Gayomart, from the light. For three thousand years Gayomart did not move or speak, but stayed in rapt contemplation of the wisdom of the creator and the perfection of the earthly paradise he had made. Then Gayomart became the first fire-priest, tending the flame that is the sign of Ahura Mazda.

Ahura Mazda creates Gayomart, who worships his maker as a fire priest

Ahriman, banished by prayer to the outer darkness, attacked creation furiously. He broke through the sky in blazing fire. He brought many things with him: lust, starvation, disease, pain, and even death, to spoil the world. He defiled everything he touched, and rejoiced as he did so. "My victory is perfect," he crowed. "I have fouled the world with filth and darkness, and made it my stronghold. I have dried up the earth, so that the plants will die, and poisoned Gayomart, so he will die."

Ahura Mazda saw that it was safer to shackle Ahriman than to let him roam free, so he set a limit to time and trapped Ahriman inside creation. Ahriman struggled as furiously to get out of the world as he had to get in, but he could not. And so he has remained in the world, doing evil until the end of time.

Ahura Mazda sent plentiful rain to end Ahriman's drought, and the rain brought forth, from Gayomart's seed, the first human couple, Mashya and Mashyoi, from whom we are all descended.

At first, Mashya and Mashyoi praised Ahura Mazda for the beauty and bounty of his creation, but then they became confused and began to praise Ahriman, even hailing him as their creator. For Ahura Mazda left all men and women free to make their own choice between what is good and what is evil.

All men are born good and the earth is happiest where one of the faithful is standing. When one of the faithful sows corn, he spreads the word of Ahura Mazda.

Therefore, Ahura Mazda made every land dear to its people and he made the lands beautiful, longing for the good and the bright. But Ahriman infected the people with sin, with disease and with sorrow.

Ahriman sends demons of suffering and death to spoil Ahura Mazda's paradise on earth

The first couple, Mashya and Mashyoi rejoice in earth's beauty – but become confused about which god created it

Mashyoi

Mashya

THE LAND OF IRAN
The continuing battle between the wise Ahura Mazda and the cruel Ahriman is reflected in the landscape and climate of Iran, from where this story originates. Barren, harsh, mountainous regions, as shown above, contrast sharply with highly fertile, coastal areas.

❖

THE FIRST MAN
Gayomart, the first man, whose name meant "Dying life" in Persian, was created by Ahura Mazda. In Persian myth, Gayomart was a spirit for 3,000 years, then took human form. He died young, however, aged only 30, poisoned by Ahriman, Ahura Mazda's evil twin.

31

THE OLD MAN OF THE ANCIENTS

THE CREATOR
Kumush, the Old Man
of the Ancients, is the
supreme god of the
Modoc tribe. He
created the whole
world, made the
Modoc's land especially
for them, his chosen
people, and scattered
seeds over it. Modoc
myth tells that Kumush
could bring a man back
to life if he had only so
much as a single hair
left on his head.

KUMUSH created the world. It was Kumush, the Old Man of the Ancients, who scattered seeds over the land, and asked the mountains, hills, rivers, and springs to care for them for ever. Kumush will never die. Nothing can kill him, for the bright disc he wears on his back always brings him back to life. Now he lives in the sky, but once he lived here, on earth.

One day, Kumush left his lodge and went wandering to the edge of the world. When he came back, he had a daughter with him. No one knows where she came from. He was away so long that, by the time he returned, all the people he had known had died.

He made his daughter ten fine dresses – one for each stage of her life. The tenth one was her burial dress. It was the most beautiful of all, made of buckskin and covered with bright shells.

Kumush makes his daughter a dress for each stage of her life

Kumush returns from the edge of the world with a daughter

A few days before she became a woman, she went into Kumush's lodge to dance. Afterwards, she fell asleep and dreamed that she was soon to die. When she awoke, she asked her father for her burial dress. He offered her each of the others in turn, but she refused them. She would only have the shroud.

As soon as she put it on, she died, and her spirit set out for the west. The sorrowful Kumush said, "I know all things above, below, and beyond. Whatever is, I know. I will follow her spirit down into the caverns of the House of Death."

Kumush's daughter puts on the most beautiful dress of all, her burial dress

The bones leap out of Kumush's basket and back into the caverns of the dead

The House of Death was beautiful and full of spirits. There were so many that if every star in the sky and all the hairs of every man and every animal were counted, they would not equal the number of spirits in that house. There Kumush stayed, dancing with the spirits.

At length, he grew weary of the House of Death, and determined to return and people the earth again. He took with him a basketful of bones, but the bones shouted and dug into him, making him stumble. Twice he fell, and twice the bones leapt out of the basket and back into the caverns below.

Kumush spoke angrily to them, saying, "Bones, be quiet! Life is good!"

At last, Kumush reached the sunlight. He took the bones from the basket and sowed them in the soil. First one tribe sprang up, then the next. Last of all were the Modocs, Kumush's chosen people. "You will be a small tribe; your enemies will be many," he said. "But you will be the bravest of all."

Then Kumush took leave of his daughter and journeyed to the edge of the world. He took the sun's road until he came to the middle of the sky. There he built his house, and there he lives still.

THE MODOC
A small tribe, living on the California-Oregon border, the Modoc were forced from their homelands in 1864. The Modoc War followed between 1872 and 1873, when for six months around 60 Modocs kept over 1000 US troops at bay – fulfilling Kumush's prophecy of the tribe's great bravery.

PRECIOUS SHELLS
Several tribes in western North America used abalone shells to decorate clothes (such as the burial dress in this story), to wear as jewellery, and to trade as money.

MADE FROM MUD

I N THE BEGINNING there was no earth, only ocean. Ulgan, the great creator, came down to make the earth, but he could not think how to do it. He saw some mud that looked as if it had a body and a face floating on the surface of the water. Ulgan brought the mud to life, called the creature Erlik, and made it his friend and companion.

One day, Ulgan and Erlik, in the shape of two black geese, were flying over the water. Erlik, who was always full of pride and boastfulness, flew too high and, exhausted, fell into the water.

Erlik began to sink. Drowning, he called out for help, and Ulgan raised him up, and also commanded a stone to rise to the surface for Erlik to sit on.

THE FROZEN NORTH
This story comes from Siberia, a vast region of Russia covering about 7,511,000 sq km (2,900,000 sq miles). Parts of it, such as Kamchatka in the east (shown above) contain treeless tundra, where the subsoil is permanently frozen. In the brief summer, the tundra has numerous mosquito-infested bogs – all, according to this tale, created by the devious Erlik.

❖

WHITE CREATOR LORD
Another name for Ulgan, used by the Yakuts who live near the river Lena in Siberia, is Yryn-ai-tojon, which means "White Creator Lord".

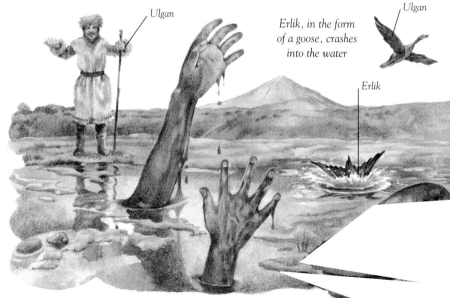

Ulgan

Erlik, in the form of a goose, crashes into the water

Ulgan

Erlik

Newly created out of mud by Ulgan the creator god, the evil Erlik rises up out of the mire

Then Ulgan asked Erlik to dive down and fetch up some mud, to make the earth. Erlik did as he was asked, but, each time, he kept some mud in his mouth, hoping to make his own world when he had seen how it was done.

Ulgan commanded the mud to expand, and the mud in Erlik's mouth obeyed. Erlik nearly choked. He spat out the mud, and that is the reason why the earth has boggy places.

Ulgan created the first man, using earth for flesh and stone for bones. Then he made the first woman out of the man's rib. But the man and woman as yet had no living spirit. Ulgan went off to look for one to give them, leaving the first dog to guard their lifeless bodies.

Erlik came and, seeing that the dog was shivering because it had no hair, he bribed the dog to look away by offering it a warm coat. Then Erlik took a reed and blew life into the bodies of the first man and woman. Thus Erlik, and not Ulgan, became the father of mankind.

When Ulgan returned and saw what had happened, he didn't know what to do. He wondered whether he should destroy the man and woman and start again. However the first frog saw Ulgan pondering this problem and told him not to worry. "If they live, let them live. If they die, let them die." So Ulgan let them live.

As for the dog, Ulgan told it that from now on it would always have to guard humankind and live out in the cold, and if it was ill-treated by humans, that was its own fault.

SIBERIAN HUSKY
Large and powerful, with great powers of endurance, the Siberian husky is used in teams for hunting and pulling sledges. This tale tells how the close partnership between dog and humans came to be forged.

Erlik bribes the first dog to look away by giving it a furry coat

Erlik

Ulgan

The frog watches as sly Erlik blows life into the first people

MYTHICAL TREE
The Yakuts believe that a mythical tree (similar to Yggdrasil, the Tree of Life in Norse myth), connects the upper world where the good Ulgan rules, the world of human beings, and the underworld, where Erlik holds sway.

Ulgan never forgave Erlik for breathing life into people. Ulgan had had enough of Erlik's sly ways, so he banished him to the underworld. There Erlik sits on a black throne, surrounded by evil spirits, who he sends out each night to carry off the souls of the dead.

CHILDREN OF THE SUN GOD

SANDPAINTING
This Navajo blanket is decorated with a sandpainting design. It shows two Holy People – perhaps White Corn Boy and Yellow Corn Girl – with the sacred maize plant, their gift to mortals. The Navajo create sandpaintings to invoke the Holy People to cure sickness among the tribe. There are over 800 different designs. Every detail of the pattern has to be correct for the sandpainting's healing power to work.

❖

SPIDER WOMAN
This wise woman teaches weaving. Spiders are protected by the Navajo, and spiders' webs are rubbed on the arms of girl babies, so that they will grow up to be tireless weavers.

THIS IS THE FIFTH WORLD. The ancestors of mankind were living in the fourth world, below this one, when a great flood came, with waves as high as mountains. The ancestors made a hole in the sky, and escaped into the world we live in now.

One day, the people heard from afar the faint "Wu'hu'hu'ú" of Hastseyalti, the talking god. Slowly the noise grew louder, until they could hear his mocasined tread, and at last he stood before them. From a piece of turquoise, he made Estsánatlehi, Changing Woman. From two ears of corn he made White Corn Boy and Yellow Corn Girl.

Changing Woman married Tsohanoai, the sun god, who carries the sun on his back and hangs it on the west wall of his house at night. He built her a home on an island far to the west, where she now lives. It is from there that the fresh breezes of spring blow and the rains come to water the Navajo country.

Changing Woman had two fine sons, Killer of Enemies and Child of Water. However, their father, the sun god, refused to have anything to do with them.

When they had grown into two strapping lads, Killer of Enemies and Child of Water decided to set out one day to find

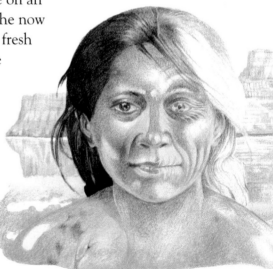

Changing Woman grows old in the winter and young again in the spring

their father and seek his help in overcoming the many evil spirits that were tormenting mankind.

They saw a plume of smoke rising from a hole in the ground, and climbed down a ladder into a chamber. There they found Spider Woman, an old crone of great wisdom. She told them how to find the sun god's house; she also gave them a special charm to keep them safe from evil, and life-feathers from the high-flying eagle.

The brothers came to the sun god's house, on the shores of a lake. The sun god was away, so they decided to surprise him. Guarding the door were two fierce bears, but the brothers spoke the Spider Woman's charm, and the bears let them pass. The brothers hid among some rugs. The rug they chose was the rug of darkness.

As soon as the sun god returned home, he sensed someone was there. He took down the rugs. First he unrolled the rug of dawn, then the blue rug of the sky, the yellow rug of the evening light, and finally, the blue-black rug of darkness.

The boys fell out. The furious sun god threw them east against the rocks of white shell; south against the rocks of turquoise; west against the rocks of mother-of-pearl; north against the black rocks. But the brothers clutched their life-feathers and were unharmed. At last the sun god's anger cooled, and he accepted the boys as his children. He gave them magic arrows to fight evil spirits – Teelget, the man-eating antelope, the Tsenhale, huge birds of prey, and Yeitso, the scaly one.

But though Killer of Enemies and Child of Water have done mighty deeds against these evil spirits, others survive. Old Age, Cold, Hunger: these can never be slain.

Bears guard the turquoise door of the sun god's house

CULTURE OF BEAUTY
As well as being superb silversmiths and makers of jewellery, the Navajo are famous for their fine rugs and blankets, woven using wool from their own sheep. Weaving is more than just a useful skill to the Navajo; the discipline, thought and controlled breathing required is a reflection of cosmic harmony.

The sun god shakes the blue-black rug of darkness and out tumble Killer of Enemies and Child of Water, his children

THE FOOD OF LIFE

CUNEIFORM TABLET
The Sumerians
invented a written
language called
cuneiform, which
means wedge or nail-
shaped. This tablet
dates from 2100 BC.

Adapa, the inventor of language, was the first of the Seven Sages sent by their father, Ea, god of wisdom, to teach people the art of living. Ea gave Adapa understanding beyond that of ordinary mortals, but only a mortal span of life.

Adapa lived with the people of the city of Eridu and taught them how to worship and to pray. He baked bread for the city and set the offering table with bread and water; it was Adapa, also, who fished the waters around the city.

Each day Adapa set out from the quay in his rudderless fishing boat. With no way of steering, he was at the mercy of the winds. One day the South Wind rose against him, threatening to overturn his boat and drown him. But Adapa said, "Strong as you are, South Wind, I am stronger!"

And Adapa cursed the South Wind and broke its wing.

For seven days the South Wind did not blow. The sky god Anu, eldest and greatest, asked, "What has happened to the wind?"

His servant Ilabrat answered, "My lord, Adapa, son of Ea, has broken its wing."

Adapa, who is out fishing in his boat, curses the South Wind and breaks its wing

Anu the sky god rose in anger from his throne and ordered Adapa to be brought before him.

Ea advised his son Adapa to approach Anu in full mourning, with his hair straggling loose and his clothes torn. "When you get to the gate of heaven," Ea added, "Tammuz will be guarding the way. He will ask you why you are in mourning. You must answer, 'I am mourning for you.' He will laugh and let you through. But do not accept any bread or water that you are offered, for they will be the bread and water of death."

Adapa followed his father's advice. Tammuz brought Adapa before Anu the sky god and spoke a word on his behalf; Adapa humbled himself before the great god, and explained that he had only broken the wing of the wind when he was threatened by a storm.

Anu listened to him, and forgave him. But still Anu's heart was heavy. "Why did Ea send you to wretched mankind, to teach them the ways of the gods? Why trouble yourself with human beings? For the life of a man is but the wink of a god's eye. Come Adapa, eat and drink the bread and water of eternal life." But Adapa refused the bread and water of life, thinking that Anu was playing a trick on him.

Adapa humbles himself before the great god Anu

"Well," said Anu, "you have made your choice. You could have lived for ever, but now you will one day die."

So Adapa returned to Eridu, full of the knowledge of death. It was his father, Ea, who had really tricked him out of eternal life, for Ea knew that mortals are creatures of time, while the gods carry on forever.

The bread and water of life

---❖---

ANU
The Sumerian god Anu was the first and most important god, the god of heaven, and ruler of the universe. He lived in the third highest heaven, far removed from mortals, but he was respected for his wise judgement and sense of justice. He was also the keeper of the bread and water of life.

Gilgamesh, page 44 ➤

Beginnings

Once given life, human beings must be taught, and their immortal teachers may be wise and helpful, or mischievous and cruel. But the price of wisdom can be great, even for the gods – as Odin discovers when he gains knowledge through suffering on Yggdrasil, the Tree of Life.

Having passed on vital knowledge to humankind, creator gods and other beings may retire to homes in the sky, or mysteriously disappear. But sometimes they become angry at people's wrongdoing and decide to destroy their own creation. Myths of a great flood, such as the one Noah survived in the Bible, are found worldwide – here, in the Sumerian story of *Gilgamesh* and the Serbian tale entitled *The Great Flood*.

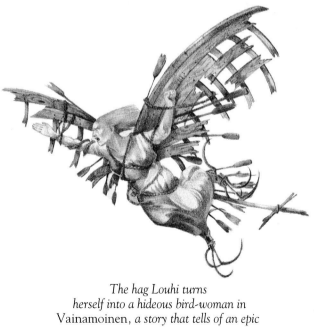

The hag Louhi turns herself into a hideous bird-woman in Vainamoinen, *a story that tells of an epic struggle to obtain a magical mill of plenty*

THE SKY WORLD

THERE ONCE WERE THREE BROTHERS and two sisters who lived up above, in the sky world. One day, Parpara, the youngest brother, went out fishing and lost a fish hook that he had borrowed from his brother Hian, who was the eldest of the three.

Hian was furious with his little brother. "I must have that fish hook!" he shouted. "Go and look for it!"

So Parpara dived into the water to search for the fish hook. After a long while, he came upon a fish, which asked him what he was looking for. Parpara explained, and the fish promised to help him. Eventually, they came across another fish, which was choking in its death-throes. Something sharp was stuck in its throat – the missing fish hook.

Parpara returned the hook to Hian, but that wasn't the end of the matter. Parpara was very angry about the bossy way his big brother had spoken to him. He decided to get his own back.

PUPPET MYTHS
Indonesia has a centuries-old tradition of shadow-puppet shows, called *wayang*. Puppets like the one above are used to dramatize all kinds of mythological tales.

ISLAND FISHERMAN
This story begins with an argument over a fish hook – in former times a valuable possession. Fishing is still carried out all around the islands of Indonesia, often by fisherman using traditional outrigger canoes.

Hian knocks into Parpara's jug of wine

A fish helps Parpara find Hian's fish hook

Parpara

Fish choking on hook

Parpara hung a jug of palm wine above Hian's bed, just where Hian was bound to knock into it when he got up.

Sure enough, Hian fell into the trap. As he got out of bed, his head smacked into the jug, which fell on to the floor, spilling its contents everywhere.

"Now look what you've done," shouted Parpara. "You've spilled all my palm wine. I want it back!"

So Hian began to scrape and dig, trying to stop the palm wine seeping into the earth. He dug so furiously that he made a hole right through to the world below.

When the brothers saw the hole, they forgot about their quarrel.

"I wonder what could be down there?" said Parpara.

"Let's see," Hian replied.

They tied a dog to a rope, and lowered it down. When they pulled it up again, the dog had pure white sand on its paws.

Intrigued, the brothers decided to discover for themselves what the world below was like. All three brothers and one of their sisters climbed down,

The brothers and sisters climb down a rope leading from the sky world into the world of human beings

each person taking a dog with them. Finally, it was the turn of the second and younger sister. As she began to descend, her brothers looking up at her made her feel nervous. She made the rope shake so much that it attracted the attention of the other people who lived in the sky world. As soon as they saw what was going on, they pulled her back up into the sky world, and the rope with her.

So Parpara, Hian, their brother and sister, and their four dogs, were trapped for ever on the world below, the world that we now live in, and they became our ancestors.

WHITE SANDS
This tale comes from the Kai Islands in southeastern Indonesia. It is not surprising that, in the story, the brothers' dog had white sand on its paws, for the islands are famous for their white sand beaches.

❖

THE FIRST MEN
The mythology of Oceania is rich and varied. Another myth from the Kai Islands relates that the first men emerged from the ground. In other Oceanic myths people are born from birds' or turtles' eggs, from a clot of blood, or from stone or wood carvings.

GILGAMESH

EPIC HERO
Gilgamesh was the hero of an epic poem first written down between 1800 and 1600 BC. This carving shows him with a lion.

G ILGAMESH, LORD OF URUK, was shaped by the gods to be a king among men. Two-thirds divine, he had perfect beauty, courage, and wisdom. He was as proud as a young bull.

Gilgamesh crossed the ocean to the edge of the sunrise. He journeyed far to find out the secrets of the world, and to bring back the story of the time before the Flood. He built the city of Uruk, where the story of Gilgamesh is carved in tablets of stone.

Now Gilgamesh was so fine in his glory that no man could stand against him, and no woman could resist him.

Aruru, the goddess of creation, decided to create a comrade for Gilgamesh. She spat into her hands, took a pinch of clay, and threw it down into the wilderness. In this way she created Enkidu, the warrior, the child of silence, the strong. His body was covered in hair like an animal; he knew nothing of mankind.

A woman from the temple of Ishtar, the goddess of love, tamed him, wild Enkidu, who was born in the hills like a falling star. She woke in his heart the thoughts of a man. She took him to Uruk, to challenge great Gilgamesh. "I am the strongest," cried Enkidu. They fought like two bulls, but at last Gilgamesh overpowered him. From struggle came friendship, closer than the love of man for woman.

Ishtar

Ishtar, the goddess of love, wants Gilgamesh to be her husband

Gilgamesh

Together, Gilgamesh and Enkidu roamed the world, for Gilgamesh had a restless heart.

Ishtar desired Gilgamesh. "Be my husband," she said, "and I will set

the world at your feet." But the hero refused, saying to her, "To which lover have you ever been faithful?"

Ishtar's desire turned to hatred. She went to her father Anu and her mother Antum. "Gilgamesh has scorned me," she said. "Father, make me a Bull of Heaven to destroy Gilgamesh. If you do not, I will break open the doors of hell and let the dead eat with the living."

Anu replied, "If I make the Bull, it will cause a seven-year drought." Ishtar told him, "Make the Bull."

Ishtar took the reins of the Bull of Heaven in her hands, and guided it to Uruk. It landed by the river, and with a snort opened up a chasm into which a hundred young men fell. It snorted again and opened up another chasm, which swallowed up another hundred young men. It snorted a third time and opened up yet another chasm. One hundred, two hundred, three hundred young men of Uruk fell into it.

Enkidu seized the Bull by its horns. As it frothed spittle into his face, he called out, "Gilgamesh, brother, strike with your sword!" Gilgamesh thrust his sword into the neck of the Bull of Heaven. He slew the Bull, and gave its heart to Shamash, the sun god.

Ishtar gave a great cry of grief at the death of the Bull and called down her curse on Enkidu and Gilgamesh. She summoned all the women of her temple to mourn over the body of the Bull of Heaven.

The next day, Enkidu told Gilgamesh, "Brother, I have had a dream. I saw the gods sitting in council. Anu and Shamash were there with Enlil of the earth and air and Ea, god of water. Anu said that, because we have killed the Bull of Heaven, one of us must die. Anu, Enlil, and Ea argued that my life should be forfeit. Shamash tried to save me, but he was only one against three. So I must die." And that very day, Enkidu fell sick.

Gilgamesh stayed at Enkidu's side during his long illness, as he wavered between life and death. One day Enkidu told Gilgamesh, "I have dreamt my death. The Black Bird of Death seized me in his talons and carried me to the House of Dust, the palace of Erkalla, Queen of the Dark." With these words, Enkidu died.

Enkidu holds the bull while Gilgamesh kills it

THE BULL OF UR
One of the treasures found at the ancient Sumerian city of Ur was this bull's head made of gold and lapis lazuli, which dates from about 2500 BC. Originally, the head decorated the sound box of a lyre.

THE GODDESS ISHTAR
This alabaster figure of the 3rd century BC represents Ishtar. As star of the morning, she was the goddess of war; as star of the evening, she was the goddess of love.

Still weeping for Enkidu, Gilgamesh roamed far and wide. "Why must we die?" he asked. "The gods live for ever, but we mortals come and go in a single breath. I will ask my ancestor Utnapishtim, whom the gods saved from the Flood, and gave eternal life."

Gilgamesh journeyed over plains and mountains, until he came to the twin peaks of Mashu, guardians of the rising and setting sun. At the gate of Mashu stand the terrible Scorpions, half man and half dragon, whose glance is death to man. But Gilgamesh was two-thirds divine.

"Why have you come to this forbidden place?" they asked.

"I have come in search of my ancestor, Utnapishtim," he replied. "I have questions for him, concerning life and death."

"No human being, or mortal thing, has trodden this road," they said. "It is the road of utter darkness. Are you not afraid?"

"Although I am afraid, still I must go in," said Gilgamesh.

And the Scorpions opened the gate.

Gilgamesh entered the dark. Dark filled his mouth and his eyes. He reached out and clutched at the dark, but it slipped through his fingers. He kept walking, while outside the sun rose and set.

And at last, Gilgamesh walked into the light, into the garden of the sun. There, by the edge of a bitter sea, Gilgamesh found the goddess of wisdom, Siduri.

Siduri told him, "You are weary, despair is in your heart. You will never find eternal life." But Gilgamesh replied, "Though I am tired, I will speak with Utnapishtim."

"No mortal has crossed this sea of death," said Siduri. "Only Shamash, the sun, can cross the ocean. Do not try. Go home. Eat, drink, rejoice. Man must die, but life is sweet."

"Where is life's sweetness, when Enkidu is dead?" asked Gilgamesh.

"Go into the forest then," said Siduri, "and seek Urshanabi, the ferryman, who will take you across the sea to Utnapishtim. But do not touch the waters of death."

Gilgamesh came at last to the home of Utnapishtim, his forefather. "I am Gilgamesh, Lord of Uruk," he said. "Far have I come, through the empty dark and across the bitter water, to ask you why men die. Enkidu, my friend, is dead, and the fear of death is upon me. Must I

At the gate of Mashu, Gilgamesh faces the Scorpions, who can kill a man at a glance

Headdresses symbolizing the sky gods, Anu and Enlil

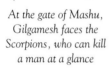

BOUNDARY STONE
In Sumeria and Babylonia, boundary stones were set up in temples or fields to record land and tax agreements. These stones were carved with symbols of the gods and goddesses who witnessed the contracts. This stone shows Anu and Enlil, the sky gods.

join him in the House of Dust? You were once a man like me. Tell me your story, Forefather."

Utnapishtim replied, "What grows, decays. The wise man and the fool both die. The dragonfly lives for the glory of the sun, then it is gone. A man grows like a reed in the river, and is cut down. Death is just like sleep, it comes to all. The gods give out the days of life, and the day of death. But I will tell you my tale."

"I lived in the city of Shurrupak, by the banks of the Euphrates, a faithful servant of the wise god Ea.

"The city grew old, and the gods grew old – Anu, the father, and his children, Enlil, Ea, Ninurta, Ennugi, Ishtar, and the rest.

"Ishtar caused trouble among men: war and unrest. The gods could not sleep for the tumult. And at last Enlil, the warrior, said to the gods, 'Let us loose the waters of the world, and drown this rabble that disturbs our rest.' And the gods agreed.

"Even Ea was bound by the gods' decision. He could not warn mankind of the flood, but he whispered the secret to my house of reeds, and the wind in the reeds whispered it to me in my sleep: 'Man of Shurrupak, tear down your house, and build a boat.'

"Obedient to the god, I built a boat, long and wide, and roofed, and took into the boat the seed of all living things. I took my family and possessions, and a male and a female of all the living creatures in the world, both wild and tame.

"For six days and six nights the tempest raged, drowning the world in a fury of wind and rain. On the seventh day, the storm calmed. I looked out from the boat, and there was nothing but water on the face of the earth. And then I wept, but that was just more water.

> ❖
>
> **UTNAPISHTIM**
> The name Utnapishtim means something like "He found life". Many aspects of his tale survive in the biblical legend of Noah, which is just one of many stories about a terrible flood or deluge.

Utnapishtim builds a boat large enough to take his family and a male and female of all the creatures in the world

CYLINDER SEAL
Before cuneiform writing, a method of recording information was to use a seal, or stamp. The cylinder seal, shaped like a cylindrical bead, was decorated with scenes that, when rolled on a piece of wet clay, produced a frieze. This cylinder seal, which dates from 2300 BC, shows the goddess Ishtar and the god Ea.

Utnapishtim gives Gilgamesh a secret to take home

While Gilgamesh washes himself in a pool, a snake eats the magic plant of youth

"Finally, the boat ran aground on the top of Mount Nisir. Eager to find out whether the flood was going down, I loosed first a dove, then a swallow, then a raven. The dove and the swallow both returned, exhausted, but the raven did not – it had found a resting place. In my joy, I made a sacrifice to the gods.

"As soon as Enlil smelled the sweet-scented smoke from my sacrifice, he was furious. 'Have some of these troublesome mortals escaped? All should have died. Someone must have warned them!'

"But wise Ea replied, 'The flood was too hard a fate for all humankind. This man, at least, did not deserve to die. However, I sent him no warning; the man had a dream.'

"At that, Enlil's anger cooled. He took me by the hand and set my wife by my side. We knelt, and he touched our foreheads. 'Until now, Utnapishtim was mortal. Now he and his wife shall be as the gods.' "

Utnapishtim looked hard at Gilgamesh. "Now, Gilgamesh, how will you persuade the gods to grant you eternal life?"

"I shall not give up," said Gilgamesh.

"Then first, you must stay awake for six days and seven nights."

As Utnapishtim spoke, sleep breathed over Gilgamesh like a fog. He slept for six days and seven nights. Each day Utnapishtim's wife placed a fresh loaf by his side. At last, Utnapishtim woke him.

"I have only been sleeping a minute," protested Gilgamesh.

"Lying man," said Utnapishtim. "Look at these loaves by your side. Today's is fresh-baked, but the others are stale and dry."

"Is there nothing I can do to become immortal?" cried Gilgamesh. "Death is stealing over me like sleep."

"You have worn yourself to nothing by journeying here," Utnapishtim replied, " so I will give you a prize to take home. On the far shore of the sea of death there grows a plant with sharp thorns like a rose. Once eaten, it will restore lost youth to a man."

Gilgamesh soon found the plant, which he called, "The Old Man Made Young Again". He took it back to Uruk, determined to try it on the old men of the city, and then on himself. But as he stopped at a pool to wash, a snake ate the plant.

Ever since, snakes have been able to shed their skins and become young again. But mankind, having once lost the plant of eternal youth, has never found it again.

THE GREAT FLOOD

ONCE, MEN LIVED IN paradise on earth. They worked only for pleasure, for everything they needed was provided for them. But they ignored the commands of God, and because of their folly he flooded the valley in which they lived, and they were drowned.

Only one man survived the terrible flood, having been set as a lookout on top of a mountain. His name was Kranyatz and he was a giant of immense strength.

Kranyatz fled higher and higher from the flood, until the water rose to the top of the highest mountain.

All there was for Kranyatz to cling on to was a vine, which was the walking stick of Kurent, the trickster god. Now although Kurent liked to play mischievous jokes and tricks on people, he had a kind side to his nature and was happy to help Kranyatz. So for nine years, until the flood receded, Kranyatz hung on to the vine and survived on its grapes and juice.

At the end of nine years, Kranyatz thanked Kurent for preserving him, but Kurent said, "It's not me you should thank, but the vine. Swear that you will always praise it, and love its juice more than any other food or drink." And Kranyatz swore.

After the flood, Kurent and Kranyatz argued about who should rule the earth. At last Kurent said, "Let us have a contest. Whoever can jump across the broad sea shall rule the earth, both on this side and the other." Kurent jumped first, and just wetted one foot on the other side of the ocean. But Kranyatz, who was far bigger and stronger than the feeble folk we see today, stepped easily across the sea, winning the first round.

Then Kurent said, "Let us see who will rule below the earth. It shall go to the stronger." And he stamped his foot and split the earth to reveal a great cavern beneath. But when Kranyatz stamped, the earth split open right to the bottom, where pure gold flows like a river.

For nine years Kranyatz clings to the vine that is Kurent's walking stick

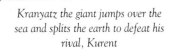

Kranyatz the giant jumps over the sea and splits the earth to defeat his rival, Kurent

BLACK HELLEBORE
Known as Christmas rose because it flowers in winter, this plant grows wild in central and southern Europe. The root was formerly used to cure cattle "troubled with cough or any poisonous thing".

"Third time pays for all," said Kurent. "Let us shoot an arrow into the sky. The one who shoots highest will rule the earth and all that is above and below."

Kurent shot, and his arrow did not come back for eight days. When Kranyatz shot, his arrow did not return for nine days, and, when it fell, the rooster who guarded God's provisions was skewered on it.

"You are emperor of the world," said sly Kurent. "I am your subject." But Kurent was thinking all the while how he could win by cunning what he had lost in the trial of strength.

Kurent squeezed his vine walking-stick and pure red juice burst out of it. He went to find Kranyatz, who was enjoying being emperor of the world, and offered him some. "Very refreshing," said Kranyatz.

Kurent went away and squeezed juice from the vine again, but this time he mixed some hellebore in with it, a plant that, when plucked by moonlight, gives visions. He found Kranyatz by the river of gold. "I'm very thirsty," said Kranyatz, "for there's no water here, only gold, and it's a seven-year walk back to the world."

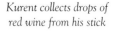

Kurent collects drops of red wine from his stick

Kranyatz shoots an arrow so high in the air it takes nine days to come down

"Have some of this, my lord," said Kurent, and Kranyatz drank. But one cup of wine was not enough to make big Kranyatz drunk, and he did not want to drink a second cup.

A third time Kurent squeezed the vine, and this time he added some of his own trickster blood to the juice. He went looking for Kranyatz once more, and found him sitting on the top of the highest mountain at God's own table, eating God's food. "If you are eating God's food, you really deserve a divine drink to accompany it," said Kurent. "Try this wine, it's the best there is."

Kranyatz drank and immediately his senses began to dim. He called for more wine and Kurent poured it, like an obedient servant. Kranyatz's head began to swim and he forgot where he was. And so God came back and found Kranyatz sitting at his table, having eaten his meat, lolling drunk amid the grease and bones.

God became angry and struck Kranyatz with his mighty hand. Kranyatz rolled down the mountain and lay there for many years, all bruised and broken. When he got well again, he was no longer strong. He could not step across the sea, or climb down to the bottom of the earth or up to heaven.

So Kurent the trickster ruled the world after all, and mankind has been feeble and weak ever since. Through the vine we were saved, and through the vine betrayed.

MOUNTAIN COUNTRY
The rugged landscape of Serbia, with its deep gorges and fast-flowing rivers, makes a suitable setting for this story of towering strength brought down to earth by low trickery.

Kurent fills Kranyatz's drinking horn with wine mixed with blood to put him into a drunken stupor

THE ORIGIN OF THE OX

THE SAGE'S MOUNT
The renowned Chinese sage Lao-Tzu, founder of Taoism, one of China's religions, began his wanderings riding upon an ox, as shown in this bronze.

❖

THE OX
The ox has a special place in Chinese myth. It is the second sign of the zodiac; people born under this sign are thought to be reliable and considerate. At various times in history, the ox has been protected by law. Many Chinese still feel that eating beef is a shameful way to repay an animal that puts its strength at the service of humans.

LONG AGO, LIFE was very hard – even harder than it is today. People had to struggle in the fields with their bare hands to grow enough food to feed themselves. They rarely had enough to eat – even though they worked day and night.

The Emperor of Heaven saw the poor people toiling on the earth and took pity on them. He summoned the Ox star from the sky, and sent it down to tell the people that if they worked hard, they would be able to eat well every third day.

The Ox rushed down to pass on the news. But it was a stupid creature, and so proud of being the Emperor's messenger, that it muddled the message. The Ox told the people that if they worked hard the Emperor of Heaven said they could have three meals a day!

The Emperor of Heaven did not want the people on earth

The Emperor of Heaven

to think that he broke his promises, so the Ox found itself yoked to the plough to till the fields. People just couldn't have done the work by themselves.

The Ox finds itself yoked to the plough to help mankind till the fields

FIRST CREATOR AND LONE MAN

IN THE BEGINNING, the surface of the earth was covered with water, and everything was dark. The First Creator and Lone Man were walking upon the surface of the water when they saw something move – a little duck.

They sent the duck diving right down to the bottom of the ocean, and it brought back some sand. First Creator and Lone Man used this sand to make the earth.

Lone man tells the tribe that the totem pole will protect them when he is gone

First Creator took the south and made the hill country, full of valleys and mountains and flowing streams. Lone Man took the north and made the plains, flat land with lakes and ponds. First Creator filled his land with game: buffalo, deer, and antelope. Lone Man made the cattle and sheep.

First Creator was not very impressed with the land Lone Man had made. "There's nowhere to hide!" he said.

But Lone Man just shrugged his shoulders. "Well, it's done now," he replied. "It's too late to change it."

Men and women peopled the land. When hard times came, Lone Man saw the people's suffering and wanted to share it. So he entered into some corn that a young girl was eating and she gave birth to him as a human being.

Lone Man was born as a man and lived with the girl's tribe. He was pure and good, and always the peacemaker in every quarrel. He never married, but the children loved him and followed him everywhere.

He taught the people many important things, but eventually it was time for him to leave them. So he instructed the tribe to set up a cedar trunk as a totem pole in the centre of the village, paint it red, and burn incense to it. "This cedar is my body," he said, " which I leave with you to protect you from all harm." And then he departed.

As for First Creator, he turned into a coyote.

CORN ON THE COB
The Mandan used to hunt buffalo and grow corn in the plains and fertile valleys of what is now North and South Dakota. Some cobs were braided into strings (as above) and dried.

VAINAMOINEN

❖

AGED HERO
Vainamoinen is born old. In another story, a girl, Aino, chooses to become a mermaid rather than marry him.

A LONG TIME THIS TALE has lain in the cold, waiting to be sung: the tale of Vainamoinen, the eternal singer. Once there was a girl made of air, nature's daughter, who lived in the empty skies. She grew bored, and went down to the blue rolling sea. The wind whipped up; the waves grew fierce. And wind and wave together made the air-girl conceive a child, Vainamoinen.

Seven hundred years she carried her unborn child. Bitterly she called out to the Old Man, who holds up the sky, to deliver her from the birth-pangs.

One day, there came a wild duck, flying here and there looking for a nesting place. It landed on the air-girl's knee, jutting out of the water. There it built its nest and laid seven eggs: six of gold, and one of iron.

As the eggs hatched, the air-girl felt as if she was on fire. She shook them off, and they smashed as they fell into the sea. From the eggs came mother earth, and the heavens above; the sun, the moon, the stars, and the clouds.

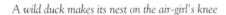
A wild duck makes its nest on the air-girl's knee

Ten summers passed; the air-girl made the islands and the mainlands; but still her child was not born.

For another thirty summers, Vainamoinen wondered what awaited him in the world outside his mother's womb. Then, calling on the sun and moon for strength, he forced his way free, and his mother the air-girl returned to the skies. Eight years the sea rocked Vainamoinen before he reached land.

The bare earth gave birth to a son, Pellervoinen, whom Vainamoinen asked to sow the land with trees and flowers. When the trees grew into forests, Vainamoinen took his axe and cleared the land to plant the first barley; however he left one birch tree for the birds to rest in. Vainamoinen prayed to the Old Woman underground to nurture the seeds, and to the Old Man in the heavens to water them. And the crops grew.

Now Vainamoinen longed for a wife and he decided to search for one in the northlands. An eagle carried Vainamoinen across the sea,

FINNISH FATHERLAND
Vainamoinen is credited with transforming barren ground to create the tree-covered landscape of the legends of the Kalevala, which means "Fatherland of Heroes".

but the winds battered him so severely that, when he arrived, he was so exhausted he could only lie on the ground and cry for his home.

Louhi, gap-toothed mistress of the north, heard him. "What would you give me, Vainamoinen," the hag asked, "to send you home again?"

He offered her gold, he offered her silver, but she would take only one thing. "I will bring you to your own land, where the cuckoo sings, if you can forge the Sampo, the mill of plenty. Beat it out of a swan's feather and a cow's milk, from a grain of barley and a sheep's wool. I will give you my beautiful daughter in return."

"I cannot forge the Sampo," said Vainamoinen, "but Ilmarinen the smith could."

"Then fetch him," grinned Louhi eagerly, "and he shall have my daughter for his wife."

Vainamoinen sang up a wind to whisk Ilmarinen the smith to the northlands, so that he could forge the magical Sampo. Three days Ilmarinen worked at his forge. He hammered and tapped, until the Sampo was made. On one side of it was a corn mill, on the second, a salt mill, and on the third, a money mill.

The hag Louhi refuses gold and silver to allow Vainamoinen to return to his homeland. Her price is far higher – the magic mill of plenty called the Sampo

Vainamoinen whistles up a wind to blow Ilmarinen the smith to the northlands, so he can forge the Sampo

Ilmarinen begins to forge the Sampo from a swan's feather

FOLK ART
This 19th-century relief sculpture from the Old University of Turku, Finland, shows Vainamoinen playing the kantele.

THE KANTELE
Vainamoinen created miraculous music from this harp-like instrument. His own kantele had a frame made from the jawbones of a horse; its strings were hairs from the horse's tail.

The hag Louhi was pleased with his work. She locked the Sampo behind nine locks and rooted it in the earth by magic. However, she sent Ilmarinen back home over the seas, in a ship of copper, without her daughter.

Determined to be revenged on Louhi, Ilmarinen and Vainamoinen decided to steal the Sampo; Lemminkainen, a resourceful young friend, returned to the north with them. Vainamoinen played sweet music on his kantele to lull Louhi to sleep and Ilmarinen smeared the nine locks with butter to ease them open. Lemminkainen then tried to pull out the Sampo, but its magic roots would not break. So he borrowed a northland ox and plough,

The monstrous whale

The Sampo

The mist-daughter shrouds Vainamoinen's ship in fog

cut through the Sampo's roots and stole away with it.

As the three comrades sailed homewards, Lemminkainen began to bellow out a song of triumph. Louhi awoke, heard his song and called on the mist-daughter to shroud the ship in fog. But Vainamoinen cut a way through the fog with his bright sword.

Louhi called up the monstrous whale to rise from the deep, but Vainamoinen sang it back down again. Then Louhi called on the Old Man in the heavens to summon up a storm. As Vainamoinen's ship struggled in the raging seas, Louhi came upon it in a ship filled with vengeful men. But into the sea Vainamoinen threw a piece of tinder that quickly grew into a hidden reef, and Louhi's ship foundered.

Louhi fastened scythes to her feet to act as claws, tied timbers from her ship's wreck to her arms to make wings and, using the ship's rudder as a tail, turned herself into a woman-bird, a mighty eagle. She flew after Vainamoinen and settled on the mast of his ship.

Vainamoinen cried, "Mistress of the North, will you not share the Sampo with us?"

"Never," she screamed.

Vainamoinen struck her with an oar, knocking her off the mast. But as she fell, she grabbed hold of the Sampo, pulling it after her.

Louhi and the Sampo hit the water and the Sampo fell to pieces.

❖

THE *KALEVALA*

The ancient legends of Vainamoinen were first collected and written down, in the form of a narrative poem called the *Kalevala*, in the early 19th century. By the time the editor, a Finnish scholar named Elias Lönnrot, had finished, the poem had over 22,000 verses. The *Kalevala* was the basis for the poem *Hiawatha*, by Longfellow.

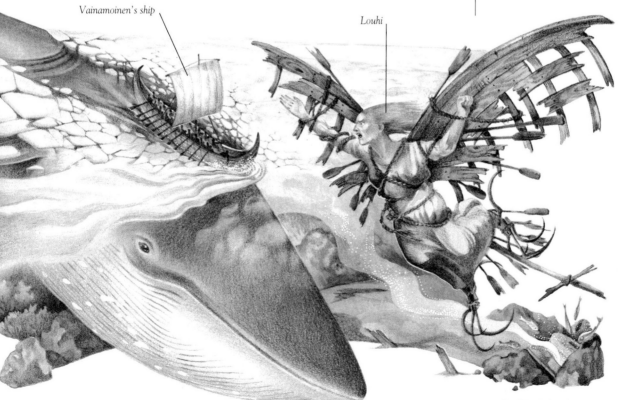

Vainamoinen's ship

Louhi

Louhi vainly tries to stop Vainamoinen's ship with fog, a whale, and by force. When her boat sinks, she becomes a terrifying eagle-woman

The corn mill and the money mill were smashed. Louhi was left with just one piece – the bare inheritance of the frozen northlands. Others, Vainamoinen gathered to enrich Finland's land. But the salt mill still rests on the sea bed, grinding out salt until the end of time.

THE GIFT OF FIRE

WHEN GREAT ZEUS overthrew his father, Cronus – as Cronus in turn had overthrown his father, Uranus – he turned against mankind. He intended to destroy the human race and start again. But he was foiled by quick-witted Prometheus.

Now the name Prometheus means "forethought", and of all the immortal Titans, Prometheus was the most clever. This was why he sided with deep-thinking Zeus against brutal Cronus and the other Titans. Although Prometheus was immortal, he was the champion of mankind; some say he even created humans from clay and water.

Prometheus gave human beings the precious gift of thought and taught people many crafts and skills, such as how to study the stars in their orbits, and how to use them to navigate the seas.

Chariot of the sun

Prometheus tricks Zeus into taking the wrong portion of ox

Prometheus teaches mankind how to study the stars

This championship of mankind angered Zeus, and his anger came to a head when Prometheus cheated the gods out of their rightful sacrifice, giving it to mankind instead. Prometheus slaughtered an ox, and divided it into two portions, wrapped in hide. The large portion was just fat and bones; the small one contained the meat. Prometheus allotted the small portion to the gods, whereupon Zeus complained. Prometheus smiled and said, "Zeus, most glorious of the gods, choose whichever you like." Of course Zeus chose the large portion. When he saw that he had been tricked, he withheld fire from mankind.

"Let them eat their meat raw," he cried.

But Prometheus outwitted him. He entered Olympus, the home of the gods, stole fire from the chariot of the sun, and carried it back to earth in a fennel plant. Then he showed mankind how to use fire to cook and keep warm. When Zeus looked down on earth and saw the glow of fires, he fell into a deadly fury.

Zeus is angry when he sees fires burning on earth

Prometheus shows mankind how to use fire to cook and keep warm

With the fire hidden in a fennel stalk, Prometheus steals away from Mount Olympus

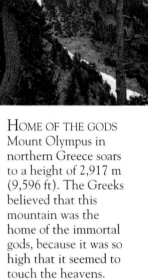

HOME OF THE GODS
Mount Olympus in northern Greece soars to a height of 2,917 m (9,596 ft). The Greeks believed that this mountain was the home of the immortal gods, because it was so high that it seemed to touch the heavens.

SWEET FENNEL
Prometheus is said to have hidden fire in a fennel stalk. Sweet fennel is popular in Greece. The leaves are used as a herb and the fleshy stalk and root is eaten as a vegetable.

Zeus took a terrible revenge on Prometheus and mankind for stealing the gift of fire. He ordered the lame smith Hephaestus to make a woman out of clay who would possess the beauty of an immortal goddess but would bring misfortune to the human race. All the gods showered her with personal gifts, and they named her Pandora, which means "all gifted".

PANDORA'S JAR
The scene on this Greek vase shows Pandora receiving gifts from the gods. Athena breathed life into her, Aphrodite gave her beauty, Apollo made her musical, Hermes taught her deceit. Pandora possessed all the contradictions of human nature.

Zeus sent Pandora as a present, not to subtle Prometheus, but to his slow-witted brother, Epimetheus, whose name means "afterthought". Prometheus had warned his brother not to accept any gift from Zeus, but Epimetheus was so enchanted by Pandora's beauty he took her for his wife.

Now Epimetheus had helped his brother distribute many gifts to mankind, and in his house he had a sealed jar that contained all the ills of disease, old age, and vice. Prometheus and Epimetheus had kept these from mankind.

Pandora couldn't help wondering what was in this jar, and one day her curiosity was too much

Pandora's curiosity gets the better of her and she opens the jar, freeing all the ills of mankind

for her. She opened the seal. Out flew all the curses of mankind, which fill our lives with suffering and misfortune. When Pandora, in her panic, replaced the lid of the jar, one thing was trapped at the bottom: Hope, who called out to her. Pandora heard the faint, sad cry and released Hope into the world to comfort mankind.

Meanwhile Zeus was planning an even crueller revenge on Prometheus. Zeus condemned him to be chained to a rock in the mountains, to endure blazing sun and freezing cold. Furthermore,

each day a long-winged eagle came to gnaw at his liver. His liver grew back again during the night, so the torment was never-ending.

But Prometheus did not give in. Although wracked with agony, he mocked Zeus, saying, "I am the only god who knows the secret that will hurl you into oblivion, like your father before you. You must release me if you wish to save yourself."

For Prometheus knew that if Zeus made love to the sea nymph Thetis, as he intended, she would bear a son stronger than his father, and Zeus's reign would end. To discover this secret, Zeus eventually allowed his own son, Heracles, to free Prometheus. In return for his freedom, Prometheus warned Zeus about Thetis, and she was married instead to a mortal, King Peleus. Their son was Achilles, a hero of the Trojan War.

ZEUS AND HEPHAESTUS
This detail from a Greek cup depicts a scene from a famous Greek myth: to cure Zeus of a terrbile headache, his son, Hephaestus, struck him with an axe; Athena sprang, in full armour, from his head.

Each day a long-winged eagle comes to gnaw at Prometheus's liver, which renews itself at night

Persephone, page 82 ➤

THE TREE OF LIFE

Huginn

O DIN THE ALL-FATHER sometimes wanders Midgard, the middle-earth, among men. He comes disguised as an old man, leaning on his staff, and he repays kindness with riches, courtesy with wisdom, and ill-treatment with vengeance.

Each morning his two ravens, Huginn and Munnin, fly forth across the world, bringing news to Odin about mankind. Odin himself can change his shape, and while his body lies as if asleep, he can travel far in the form of a bird or beast, unknown to men.

Munnin

Many stories are told of how the All-Father gained his great wisdom and his magical powers. But for every gain, there was a price to pay.

The world tree, Yggdrasil, is a gigantic ash that towers over the world. One root is in the dread realm of Niflheim, where the serpent Nidhogg feeds on corpses, and gnaws at Yggdrasil itself. A second root is in the gods' realm of Asgard, and here dwell the Norns, three old women who rule the destinies of men. Their names are Fate, Being, and Necessity, and they keep Yggdrasil alive by sprinkling the root with pure water from the well of fate. The third root lies in Jotunheim, the land of the giants. Beneath this root is the well where the severed head of wise Mimir speaks hard words. Odin paid with one of his eyes to drink insight and knowledge from that well.

But it was on Yggdrasil itself that the High One, the All-Father, the Hooded One, the terrible Spear-Shaker, Odin of the many names, gained the secret of the runes, magic symbols by which men can record and understand their lives. For nine long nights Odin hung on the windswept tree, pierced with a spear, offering himself in sacrifice. Not even Ratatosk, the squirrel that runs up and down the tree carrying insults from the eagle at the top to the serpent Nidhogg at the bottom, offered him food or drink. At the end of his ordeal, Odin gave a great cry and, seizing the runes, fell from the tree.

When he rose again from death, Odin knew many things hidden from man. He knew how to heal the sick; he knew how to blunt his enemy's blade, and how to catch an arrow in its flight.

ONE-EYED GOD
This one-eyed figure is thought to be Odin, god of war and wisdom, and the most powerful god of Norse myth. Odin wanted to know all things, so he exchanged one of his eyes for knowledge. Then he offered himself as a sacrifice to gain the secret of the runes, or magic spells.

❖

HUGINN AND MUNNIN
Odin's constant companions were two ravens, Huginn and Munnin, whose names mean "thought" and "memory". These two birds, who fed off the bodies of the dead on the battlefield, brought information to Odin, whispering it in his ear.

◄ *Out of the Ice, page 18*

Eagle

Ratatosk

Yggdrasil

Nidhogg, in Niflheim

The Norns, in Asgard

Mimir, in Jotunheim

*For nine nights Odin hung on the tree of life, pierced through with
a spear, until, at long last, he gained the secret of the runes*

God of gods, god of battles, Odin holds mankind in his care.
To poets he gives sips of the mead of poetry brewed long ago by
the dwarfs; to warriors slain in battle, he gives a lordly welcome
in the golden halls of Valhalla.

TREE ARMLET
This 10th-century gold
armlet from Rabylille in
Denmark is engraved
with the tree of life,
Yggdrasil. This giant
ash tree had three roots,
each one in a different
world. The highest,
Asgard, was where the
gods lived; on the next
level was Jotunheim,
the realm of the giants;
at the bottom was
Niflheim, the land of
the dead.

Loki the Trickster, page 64 ➤

LOKI THE TRICKSTER

FREYJA THE BEAUTIFUL
The Norse goddess of magic, fertility, and love, Freyja was so beautiful that all ornaments were named after her. This Viking pendant representing Freyja shows the necklace Brisingamen, around her shoulders.

T HE NORSE GODS were troubled in the high realm of Asgard. Their home had no wall to protect them from enemies. So when a horseman came and offered to build a wall, they listened eagerly.

"It will be a great wall," he said, "a barrier to all your foes. In eighteen months from now, all your worries will be over."

"And what is your price?" asked Odin the wise.

"Nothing less than the goddess Freyja as my wife," replied the stranger. "And the sun and moon, too."

The gods were furious, and would have thrown the man out of Asgard for daring to think that the beautiful Freyja could be bartered for building work. But cunning Loki said, "If you can build the wall in six months, it's a deal." To the other gods, he whispered, "In six months he can only build half a wall, but at least that'll be free."

The builder took one more look at Freyja, as she wept tears of gold, and agreed, as long as his horse was allowed to help him.

All through the winter the stranger worked. With the help of his horse he managed to quarry the stone for a massive wall around Asgard.

As Loki plots and Freyja weeps, the builder starts to make a wall around Asgard

Odin

Thor

Loki

Freyja

As summer approached, disaster stared the gods in the face. For, against all odds, the builder had nearly completed the wall.

"You think you're so clever, Loki," said Odin. "You got us into this; you must get us out. We cannot let Freyja marry this stranger, who must be a giant in disguise. And without the sun and moon, life will scarcely be worth living. Do something!"

So Loki thought hard, and finally he said, "Without the horse, the builder could not haul the rocks to complete his work."

Now Loki was able to change his shape, and that night, disguised as a pretty mare, he lured away the builder's horse.

VIKING SLEDGE
This sledge is part of Viking burial treasure found at Oseberg in Norway. It has curved oak runners and a decorated open box. This type of sledge was used by the Norse people for transporting goods over ice or snow.

The builder's horse is lured into the woods by Loki, disguised as a mare

Thor strikes the builder with his hammer, Miollnir

Realizing he could not complete the wall in time, the builder became enraged. His disguise fell away, revealing him as a giant, one of the gods' foes. The gods called for Thor, the strongest of them all. With his hammer, Miollnir, Thor paid the builder his wages: not the sun and the moon, but a thunderclap on the head.

As for Loki, when he next thought it safe to show his face in Asgard, he was leading a strange horse with eight legs, whose name was Sleipnir. Loki gave Sleipnir to Odin, saying, "No horse will ever keep pace with this one. He will bear you over the sea and through the air, and to the land of the dead and back." As Loki promised, Sleipnir never failed his new master, Odin.

Loki and Sleipnir

Not all of Loki's offspring are like Sleipnir. Loki himself is half giant, and he has three children by a giantess. The first is the Fenris-wolf, who at the end of the world will devour Odin. The second is the Midgard serpent, and the third is the mistress of death, Hel, who feasts on hunger and thrives on sickness.

The Midgard serpent is so enormous that it encircles the world and bites its own tail

Hel, one of Loki's terrible children, feasts on hunger and thrives on sickness

FROZEN LANDSCAPE
The Norse people lived in lands of glaciers and icefields, and these features are reflected in their myths and sagas.

When Odin realized that these terrible children were loose in the world, he had them brought to him. The serpent he threw into the ocean; it was so huge it encircled the world and bit its own tail. Hel he banished to Niflheim, the Land of the Dead, and gave her power over all who die of illness or old age.

However, the Fenris-wolf was not so easily managed. Only the god Tyr was brave enough to feed it, and even he could see that the Fenris-wolf would soon grow strong enough to do terrible harm. So the gods made a strong chain and tied the wolf up. But with one kick it smashed the links. They tried again with an even stronger chain. Once again the wolf broke free.

Finally Odin asked the dwarfs for help, and they made the fetter called Gleipnir. Silky soft, Gleipnir was made of special ingredients: the sound of a cat's footfall; a woman's beard; a mountain's roots; a bear's sinews; a fish's breath; and a bird's spittle.

The gods took the Fenris-wolf to a lonely island, and challenged it to break Gleipnir. Sensing a trap, the wolf agreed to be bound only if one of the gods would put a hand in its mouth, as a token of good faith. So brave Tyr thrust his hand into the wolf's fearsome jaws.

They bound the wolf with the silken fetter, and this time

❖

TYR THE BRAVE
The god Tyr was courageous and daring, which is why he agreed to put his hand into the Fenris-wolf's mouth. He was also a war god and helped establish basic rules for fighting. Swords were often marked with a T for Tyr, which was said to bring victory in battle. Tuesday is named after the god Tyr.

The Fenris-wolf   *Tyr*

The gods bind the Fenris-wolf with the magic fetter, and Tyr puts his hand into its mouth

when he kicked, the fetter only tightened. Furious, the Fenris-wolf clamped its great jaws together, and bit off the god Tyr's right hand.

Even though they knew that the time would come when the Fenris-wolf would break free and bring death and destruction to them all, the gods did not kill it. "What must be, will be," they said.

❖

GLEIPNIR
The magic fetter Gleipnir was as soft as a silk ribbon, but it was much stronger than any metal chain.

The Apples of Youth, page 72 ➤

MAUI-OF-A-THOUSAND-TRICKS

MAUI
The trickster hero of Polynesian culture was born a premature weakling. His mother, Taranga, threw him into the sea, but he survived and grew to be a hero. This story tells of just two of his many feats of cunning and strength: fishing up islands from the sea and slowing down the sun to make daytime last longer.

MANY ARE THE STORIES of Maui-of-a-Thousand-Tricks, who fished up the islands of the South Seas from the bottom of the ocean. Maui also went down into the Underworld and brought back the secret of fire for mankind.

One day Maui said, "The days are too short – there's no time to get anything done!"

Maui set to thinking how the sun could be made to move more slowly across the sky. From coconut-shell fibres, he made a great noose with which to catch the sun, but the sun burned it up.

Then Maui cut off the sacred tresses of his wife, Hina, and wove them into a rope, fashioning the end into a noose. He travelled to the eastern edge of the sea and waited for the sun to rise.

Maui fishes up islands from the sea bed

With a rope made from his wife Hina's tresses, Maui lassoes the sun

At dawn, Maui flung his rope and caught the sun by the throat! The sun struggled and pleaded, but Maui refused to let it go. Eventually the sun grew so weak it could no longer run across the sky, but only creep. In this way Maui brought humans more hours of light.

HUNTING THE SUN

BAMAPAMA WAS A CRAZY MAN in the Dreamtime. He was a robber and a no-good, always getting into trouble – usually for chasing after girls. He used to live underground, in the country where the sun never goes down but just hangs in one place.

One time, he decided to go above ground, saying, "I think I'll go hunting." When he got to the surface he saw a beautiful, big kangaroo. Bamapama took his spear and gave chase but the kangaroo ran off towards the west. As the kangaroo ran away, so, little by little, the sun went down.

At last the kangaroo stopped running and Bamapama took aim with his spear. But just as he was about to throw it, the sun disappeared completely and night fell. Never having known darkness, Bamapama was very afraid and began to cry. He climbed a tree to see if he could get above the darkness, but to no avail. He climbed down and, tired out, fell asleep on the ground. When he awoke next morning, to his joy he found that it was light again.

When he saw the sun, he said, "This is a good way they do things up here – sleeping at night and getting up with the sun."

When he got home, everyone asked him, "What happened to you?"

"I was chasing this big kangaroo," he said, "and then everything went dark. Come up with me and see. Everything is different up there. The sun comes up in the day, but at night you sleep. It's a good way."

He took all the people up to the surface. When it grew dark, they too were afraid and climbed up trees, but he coaxed them down. "Don't be afraid," he said. "I know what I'm doing."

In the morning the sun rose, and they stretched in the warmth. "This is good!" they said. "This is better than living down below, where it is so hot all the time. And there's wood to make fires if we get cold. Let's stay."

So Bamapama's people stayed on the surface. But they are not like us. They have no mouths, just an opening in the top of their heads. One of them once went to look for a honey bees' nest. He filled a basket with the honey, then put it on his head. He made a hole in the bottom of it so that the honey would drip down into his stomach. They're all like that.

KANGAROO
This was one of the main animals hunted for food by Aboriginals and is the subject of many paintings. The stripes on the kangaroo represent different clans.

Bamapama ventures above ground to hunt

THE SKY GOD'S STORIES

KWAKU-ANANSE the spider once went to the sky god Nyankonpon to try to buy his stories. The sky god said, "What makes you think you could buy my stories? The richest villages have all tried, and have all failed."

Kwaku-Ananse asked, "What is the price?"

"The price is Onini the python; Osebo the leopard; Mmoboro the hornet swarm; and Mmoatia the spirit."

The spider replied, "I will bring you all these things and my mother Nsia, too."

The spider went home and told his mother, Nsia, and his wife, Aso, what the sky god had said. "How can I catch Onini?" he asked.

"Go and cut a branch from a palm tree and some creeper, and bring them to the stream," said Aso.

Kwaku-Ananse did as he was told, and then he and Aso began to argue over the branch. "It's longer than he is," said Aso.

"You lie," replied Ananse. "He is longer."

The python overheard and, overcome with curiosity, asked what the quarrel was about. Ananse replied, "My wife, Aso, says that this palm branch is longer than you and I say it is not."

So Onini the python stretched himself full length along the branch and, as he did so, Ananse trussed him tight with the creeper, all the way up to his head.

PLANTAIN Larger than a sweet banana, a plantain, or cooking banana, is popular in African and West Indian cooking. The large leaves of the plantain are often used to protect food when it is steamed. In this story, Ananse the spider pretends to shelter from the rain under a plantain leaf.

As the python stretches himself along the branch, Ananse ties him to it with creeper

Then they turned their attention to Mmoboro the hornet swarm. Aso told Ananse what to do. He cut a gourd and filled it with water, and carried it to where he could see the swarm hanging from a

Ananse shelters under a plantain leaf

branch. He spilled half of the water on the hornets, and half on himself. Then he cut a plantain leaf and put it on his head, calling out, "Hornets! It is raining! I am sheltering under this leaf, but you have no protection. Why don't you come into this gourd to keep dry?"

So the hornets flew into the gourd, and Ananse slapped the plantain leaf over the opening and trapped them inside.

The hornets fly into the gourd

The leopard is caught in the pit

Then Aso told Ananse to dig a pit, and he did so. He dug it on the path between Osebo the leopard's lair and the stream, and covered it with leaves. At first light he went to the pit and there, helpless inside, was the leopard.

Ananse carves a doll from wood

There remained the spirit, Mmoatia, to catch. Aso and Ananse carved a doll from wood and plastered it with sticky gum from a tree. Then they set the doll down where the tree spirits play, with a brass basin beside it containing an appetizing mash of yams. When the spirits came, Mmoatia saw the doll, and asked it, "Can I have some yams?" The doll did not reply. So the spirit slapped the doll's cheek, and her hand stuck fast. She slapped it again; her other hand stuck, too.

Then Ananse went to the sky god with Onini the python, Osebo the leopard, Mmoboro the hornet swarm, Mmoatia the spirit, and Nsia, his old mother. The sky god called all the other gods to him, saying, "See! Great kings have come seeking my stories, but were not able to buy them. But Kwaku-Ananse has paid the price and added his mother, too. Therefore, today and forever I make a gift of my stories to Ananse the spider, and now they shall be known as Spider Stories!"

The sky god gives his stories to Ananse the spider

GOURDS
These fleshy fruits with hard skins come in many shapes and sizes, the most common being the bottle gourd. Gourds can be hollowed out and used as containers.

THE APPLES OF YOUTH

Loki's capacity for getting into trouble, and then getting out of it with his quick wits, means no one can feel really safe when he is around. He is easily bored, and so is always making mischief. Once, he nearly cost the gods their youth. It was like this.

One day, he and Odin were travelling through the wilderness. They were hungry, and so they killed an ox and made an oven in the earth to cook it in. But however long they waited, getting hungrier and hungrier, the meal just would not cook. They heard laughter above them, and when they looked up they saw a great eagle sitting in a tree. The eagle told them it was to blame for their trouble. "If you let me eat my fill of the ox, then it will cook." The gods agreed. The eagle dropped down from the tree just as the smell of cooked meat began to fill the air, and started to devour the ox. Loki and Odin could see that soon there would be nothing left. So Loki, in a temper, picked up a pole from the ground and struck the eagle with it.

The pole stuck fast to the eagle – and also to Loki's hands. When the eagle flew away, it dragged Loki into the air behind it.

GOLDEN EAGLE
In this story the giant Thiassi disguises himself as an eagle in order to eat the ox, and then carry off Idun and her apples. Loki disguises himself as another bird of prey – a falcon – to rescue Idun and bring her back to Asgard. The golden eagle, above, is the largest bird of prey in Northern Europe. It is a strong and skilful flier, with a wingspan of over 2 m (over 6 ft). It swoops down on its prey and carries it off in its powerful talons.

❖

THIASSI
The giant Thiassi took great pleasure in teasing and tormenting the gods. Like most giants in Norse myths, he was a master of deception and disguise, but in the end he could not get the better of mighty gods such as Odin.

Odin and Loki look up to see an eagle in the tree, laughing at them

Loki pleaded to be let go, but the eagle – who was the giant Thiassi in disguise – said, "I'll only release you if you promise me the goddess Idun and her Apples of Youth, which keep the gods forever young." Loki agreed.

Loki returned to Asgard and told Idun that he had found some wonderful apples in the forest, better even than the Apples of Youth.

The eagle drags Loki behind it

"Bring your apples with you, and come and compare them to the ones I've found," he said. So he lured Idun out of Asgard, in order that the giant Thiassi could come in eagle shape and steal her away.

Without Idun and her apples the gods became grey and old. "What has become of her?" they asked. And then someone remembered seeing her outside Asgard with Loki.

Loki tricks Idun into leaving Asgard with the Apples of Youth

So the gods brought Loki before them, and threatened him with a thousand painful deaths if he didn't bring Idun back.

"I can do it," he said, "if I can use Freyja's falcon shape."

So Loki flew in the shape of a falcon to Thiassi's mountain, where he found Idun alone.

The gods, who have grown old and grey, question Loki about Idun's disappearance

MAGIC APPLES
Idun, the wife of Bragi, was the keeper of the Apples of Youth, which kept the gods from growing old. Idun was the personification of youth and beauty. Her trusting nature made it easy for Loki to trick her into taking the apples out of Asgard. In both Norse and Greek mythology, apples are associated with eternal youth.

He changed Idun into a nut and, holding her in his falcon's claws, flew back to Asgard as fast as he could. But Thiassi followed him in eagle shape, and the beating of his great wings whipped up a fierce storm behind them.

The gods saw the storm and knew that Thiassi was on his way. They prepared a bonfire inside the wall of Asgard, and as soon as Loki had landed, they set light to it. Thiassi flew straight into the fire and burned his feathers. Then the gods killed him, for daring to steal Idun. Odin threw Thiassi's eyes into the sky, where they still shine as stars.

Thiassi burns in the fire, and Odin throws the giant's eyes into the sky

Thor in the Land of Giants, page 118 ➤

EARTH-MAKER AND COYOTE

THE COYOTE
A relative of the jackal family, the coyote ranges widely over North America. Smaller than a wolf, it is adaptable and cunning. Attempts to eradicate it, by poison, shooting, or trapping, have been largely ineffective. The coyote seems indestructible – just like the character in this story.

❖

TRICKSTER GOD
Coyote is the trickster god of the tribes of the southwestern USA. In this myth, from the Maidu of California, Coyote is cunning and destructive, a bringer of sickness, sorrow, and death. Sometimes, however, Coyote is a bringer of benefits. For example, the Lakota Sioux have a story about him creating the horse.

WHEN THIS WORLD was just covered water, Earth-maker floated on the surface. Coyote was with him; they were the first two chiefs. When Earth-maker sang this world into being, he said, "Let the world be good!"

But Coyote replied, "No!"

Every good thing Earth-maker said, Coyote contradicted. For instance, after he had made men, Earth-maker said, "When they die, they shall come back to life."

But Coyote said, "Why? When they are dead, they should stay dead. I am the oldest, and what I say goes."

Now Coyote had a son, a good boy, who had never left the house. One day, Coyote said to him, "Go to the stream and fetch some water." When the boy got to the stream, the rushes turned into rattlesnakes and bit him, and he died.

"What have I done?" moaned Coyote. "I take it all back. Death was

Earth-maker

Coyote

By the stream, the rushes turn into rattlesnakes and kill Coyote's son

a bad idea." He pleaded with Earth-maker, "Make him come alive again, and I will agree with everything you say."

But it was too late, Earth-maker could not undo what had occurred. Angry and bitter, Coyote started to travel around the world, and everywhere he went he made mischief, scratching up the soil and causing havoc. Earth-maker said, "People, if you see Coyote, kill him. He is bad all through. I wanted to make the world good, but he has thwarted me."

The people, heeding Earth-maker, went in search of Coyote. Eventually they cornered him on a little island. "You can stay there and starve," they said. Earth-maker told them that if after four days they heard no howling, then Coyote was dead.

But Coyote escaped by making himself like fog and drifting across the water to land. Then he howled fit to make the people's hair stand on end. So they knew he was not dead.

Every time the people tried to kill him, Coyote escaped. So Earth-maker told them to make a big canoe and get in it, and then he flooded the world. At the last minute, Coyote slipped into the canoe.

DANCE PLUME
The Maidu are very skilled at creating garments, such as headbands, cloaks, and blankets, from feathers. These are often used in ceremonial dances.

To avoid being starved to death on an island, Coyote makes himself like fog and drifts away

After the flood, Coyote escapes from the canoe on to a mountain peak, becoming an everlasting trouble to humankind

He was disguised, and no one knew he was there until they sighted land – the peak of Canoe Mountain, poking out of the water. Coyote leapt from the boat, bold as brass, saying, "This land is mine."

Earth-maker said, "Brother, you are too powerful. I can't kill you. You have won."

And Coyote is still in the world, causing trouble wherever he goes.

MAKE ME A MAN!

MAN OF IRON
The king asks the smith Walukaga to make him an iron man, perhaps similar to this statue of the war god Ebo, made by the Fon tribe of Bénin, West Africa.

L ONG, LONG AGO there was a king who called Walukaga, chief of the metal smiths, to him. "Make me a man!" the king commanded. Walukaga said, "But –"

"But me no buts," interrupted the king. "Here is all the iron you'll need. But mind, it must be a real, living, breathing man, with blood in his body and brains in his head."

Walukaga took the iron and went sorrowfully home. He asked all his friends, but none of them had the slightest idea how to make a real man. But Walukaga knew that, if he failed to create a man, he and his whole family would be severely punished – even killed.

One day, as he walked along pondering this hopeless situation, Walukaga met an old friend who had gone mad and lived alone in the wilderness. Walukaga told this madman his troubles, and the madman – who was not as crazy as he seemed – told Walukaga what to do.

With the madman's wise words ringing in his ears, Walukaga went to the king and said, "I've gone into this business of making a man and it can be done. But first, your majesty, you must order all the people to shave their heads and burn their hair, to make a thousand loads of charcoal. Then you must make them collect one hundred large pots full of tears to quench the fire while I am forging the man. For, of course, ordinary charcoal from wood and ordinary water from a stream are no use at all for making a man!"

The king orders his people to shave their heads and burn their hair, and to collect 100 pots of their tears, so that Walukaga can create a living man from pieces of iron

The king did as Walukaga asked. All the people had to shave their heads and burn their hair, but all their efforts only produced one load of charcoal. They all wept until their eyes were dry, but they only produced two pots of water.

So the king had to send once more for Walukaga. "Do not trouble to make the man," he said, "for I cannot supply the charcoal or the water."

"Your majesty," replied Walukaga, "I am glad that you could not find enough hair or enough tears, for, to tell the truth, I could not make you a man!"

WHY DO WE DIE?

CHUKU, THE GREAT SPIRIT, created the world and humankind. He sent a dog to the first people to tell them that, if anyone died, they should lay the body upon the earth and sprinkle it with ashes, and then the person would come back to life. But the dog dawdled on the way, so Chuku sent a sheep with the same message.

When the sheep arrived, it had forgotten what it was supposed to say. It got the message all muddled, and said that if anyone died, the body should be buried in the earth.

When the dog eventually arrived, it was too late. No one would believe him. "We have been told to bury the dead, and that is what we shall do," the first men said. So death came to humankind.

❖

THE GREAT SPIRIT Chuku, whose name means "Great Spirit", is the supreme god of the Ibo of southeastern Nigeria, West Africa. Chuku is the creator of all things, and all good things flow from him. His daughter is Ale, the goddess of the earth.

Chuku, the Great Spirit, sends a dog with a vital message: how to bring a dead person back to life

When the dog is late, Chuku sends a sheep. But the sheep gets the message wrong

CULTURAL CENTRE
A large country with great contrasts in landscape, ranging from tropical rainforest to grasslands, Nigeria has been a centre of African culture since 500 BC. There are four main tribes. The Ibo, who tell this tale, live in the southeast; the Hausa and Fulani live in the north, and the Yoruba in the south.

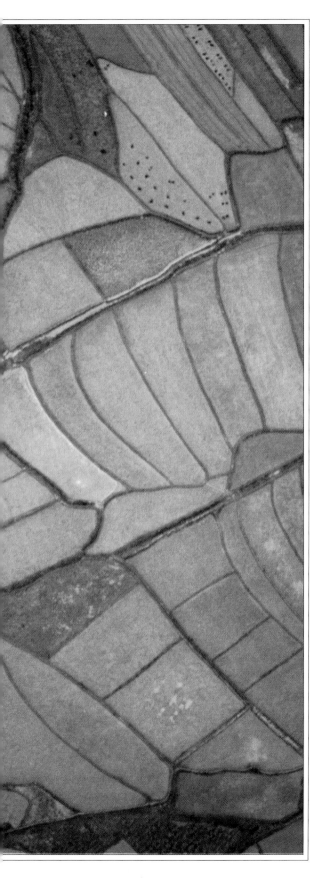

FERTILITY AND CULTIVATION

Many myths seek to explain the everyday miracles of life: the rising and setting of the sun, the growth of crops, the births of babies. Sometimes a god of fertility or farming may become angry, like Telepinu, and require appeasing, or, like Osiris, be sacrificed to enrich the land. A nervous sun goddess, Amaterasu, may have to be enticed out of a dark cave so that crops will grow, or an act of great courage may be required to bring fertility to a blighted land.

The medieval tales of King Arthur touch on these themes. Arthur inherits a riven land, and unites it. His knights then have to embark on a spiritual quest in search of a lost Christian relic, the Holy Grail. Only when the purest of Arthur's knights, Sir Galahad, has found the Grail can the wasteland kingdom bloom again.

A cow shows Cadmus where to build a great city in Cadmus and the Sown Men, *which also tells of warriors springing up from the earth and founding a proud race*

ISIS AND OSIRIS

SPIRIT OF CREATION
Osiris, god of the Underworld, was tall, handsome and dark-skinned. His followers looked forward to a life of eternal bliss. He was also the god of creation and the fertile earth.

Geb

T HE SKY GODDESS NUT and her husband, the earth god Geb, were so close that nothing could exist between them; nor could Nut's children be born. So Shu, their father, separated them, holding Nut's body aloft so that living things could exist on the earth. Nut brought forth two sets of twins: Osiris and Isis, and Set and Nepthys. Isis and Osiris loved each other, but Nepthys hated Set; she, too, loved Osiris.

At the birth of Osiris a voice was heard all over the world, saying, "The lord of all the earth is born!" Osiris became King of Egypt and ruled wisely with Isis as his queen. He established the laws, taught the people how to grow food and how to worship the gods.

Osiris had only one enemy: his jealous brother, Set. Set secretly measured Osiris's body, and made a painted coffin to fit him exactly.

Shu holds the body of Nut the sky goddess aloft so that life can exist on earth

Osiris fits perfectly into the coffin that his brother Set has made for him

SPIRIT OF DECAY
According to myth, Set had pale skin and red hair – which indicated an evil character to the Egyptians. Set is the eternal enemy of the life-affirming Osiris.

Then he gave a feast, to which he invited his brother. He showed off the magnificent coffin and said that he would give it as a present to whoever fit inside it.

All the guests took turns to lie down in the coffin, but they were all too small. At last Osiris himself lay down; his body fit perfectly. Then Set and his friends nailed down the lid, poured boiling lead over it to seal it, and set the coffin adrift on the River Nile.

When Isis heard what had happened to her husband, she was stricken with grief. She cut off her long hair, dressed in mourning, and set off in search of the coffin. No one she asked could tell her what had become of it; but at last some children playing by the river told her where it lay.

Isis brought the coffin back to her palace, and summoned the jackal-headed god Anubis to embalm Osiris's body. But first she turned herself into a sparrowhawk and, hovering over Osiris, fanned breath into his body with her wings. She revived him for long enough to conceive a son, Horus. Then she hid the child from the wrath of Set.

Set, hunting in the moonlight, came upon the opened coffin and, in his rage, tore the body of Osiris into fourteen pieces, which he scattered all over the country.

Isis travelled all over Egypt in a boat of papyrus reeds, gathering up the corpse of Osiris and burying each piece where she found it.

ANUBIS
This Egyptian god with the head of a jackal presided over funerals and was known as "Lord of Mummy Wrappings".

Children tell Isis where to find the painted coffin

Anubis prepares Osiris's body for burial

Isis turns into a hawk to fan life into Osiris's corpse with her wings

Osiris rules the land of the dead

In her reed boat, Isis searches for the pieces of Osiris's body. She buries them wherever she finds them to bring goodness to the land

Osiris went to rule the other land, where he judges the souls of the newly dead. But when his son Horus grew to adulthood, Osiris momentarily returned to ask him to avenge his death. So Horus and Set began their eternal struggle of good and evil. Sometimes one seems to win and sometimes the other, but neither can be vanquished. It is said that when Horus finally overcomes Set, Osiris will return to the land of the living to rule as king once again.

❖

GOD OF THE SKY
Horus, the sky god, is depicted with a falcon's head. Many Egyptians believed the sky was a vast falcon; its two eyes were the sun and moon.

PERSEPHONE

PERSEPHONE IS THE daughter of Demeter, goddess of the cornfield. As a young girl she was known as Core, the maiden, but now she is called Persephone, Queen of the Underworld, and each time she cuts a hair from her head, someone dies. This is what happened.

One day, Core was picking flowers in a meadow, when the ground opened up at her feet. Out of the gaping earth drove fierce Hades, King of the Underworld, in his great chariot drawn by four jet-black stallions. Hades had loved Core from a distance, and had brooded in his dark kingdom over her bright beauty. In an instant he seized her, pulled her into his chariot, and dragged her down with him.

Her screams still echoed in the air above the chasm, but Core was gone.

Core scatters her flowers in terror as the earth opens

Hades, King of the Underworld, seizes Core and pulls her into his chariot

Hades's chariot disappears into the depths of the dark Underworld

THE SEASONS
Demeter, the goddess of the cornfield, was responsible for the harvest of all crops, flowers, and plants. When she lost her daughter, she forbade anything to grow on the earth. Winter fell when Persephone was in the Underworld; when she came back to earth, it was summer again.

Demeter, her mother, heard her cries. Dressing herself in mourning, she lit two torches at fiery Mount Etna and, with one in each hand, she wandered the world for nine days and nights, neither eating nor drinking, calling for her daughter. But no answer came.

At last Demeter came to Helios, the sun, who had seen everything. "It is no use calling," he said. "Your daughter Core is now the bride of Hades. She is no longer a maid; her new name is Persephone."

Demeter had been the gentlest of all gods and goddesses, but at this news she let out a terrible cry. She turned her anger on the world, and forbade the flowers to bloom or the crops to grow. Soon the earth became a wasteland. The gods begged Demeter to relent, but she would not. At last Zeus ordered Hades to give up the girl, provided she had not eaten the food of the dead. Persephone had eaten nothing but six pomegranate seeds given to her by the gardener Ascalaphus, so Hades was forced to agree.

Demeter wanders the world calling for her daughter

As Demeter greets her long-lost daughter, winter fades and the world becomes green again

In her underground prison, Persephone eats six pomegranate seeds

Ascalaphus

POMEGRANATE SEEDS Persephone could not leave the Underworld forever because she had eaten the pomegranate seeds from Hades's garden. Some say it was Hades's gardener, Ascalaphus, who saw Persephone eat the seeds. The pomegranate is a thick-skinned fruit with seeds floating in a juicy pulp. The tree grows in Mediterranean countries, and in other parts of the world that have a hot, dry climate.

When Persephone reached the upper world, she ran to embrace her mother. Demeter's anger melted, and the world became green again.

Zeus told Persephone that each year she must spend six months in the Underworld, as the bride of Hades, one winter month for each seed that she had eaten. But for the other six months, of spring and summer, she could return to the living world, to be with her mother.

Cadmus and the Sown Men, page 96 ➤

WORLD WITHOUT SUN

SWORD GUARD
This 19th-century Japanese sword guard, made of silver inlaid with gold, shows the Buddhist god Kannon riding on the back of a carp. Kannon is a merciful god, who sailors believe protects them from shipwreck.

UZUME
The goddess of mirth lures Amaterasu the sun goddess from her cave, restoring light to the world. This figurine stands just over 13 cm (5.2 in) high and is made of wood with an ivory face.

WHEN THE GOD IZANAGI gave birth to the sun goddess Amaterasu, the moon god Tsuki-yomi, and the storm god Susanowo, he was so pleased with his offspring that he divided up the world between them. To Amaterasu he gave the rule of the High Plains of Heaven. To Tsuki-yomi he entrusted the realms of the night. And to Susanowo he gave the rule of the oceans.

But while Amaterasu and Tsuki-yomi were pleased, Susanowo screamed and howled, and complained that he did not want to rule the oceans. "I'd rather have been given charge of Yomi, the Land of Gloom," he said. But that was the province of Izanami, goddess of death and decay.

So instead of looking after the oceans, Susanowo just hung around in heaven and on earth, causing trouble wherever he went. He uprooted trees, destroyed rice paddies, and knocked down buildings. Finally he skinned a dappled pony in the heavens, and dropped it through the thatched roof of the sacred weaving hall, where Amaterasu and her maidens were at work, weaving the world into pattern and order.

Amaterasu was so shocked and terrified that she fled. She shut herself inside a cave and wouldn't come out. The whole world, both heaven and earth, was plunged into darkness. Nothing would grow, and soon chaos reigned.

Disgusted at only being given rule over the sea, Susanowo, the storm god, wreaks havoc

The gods decided that they would have to lure Amaterasu from her hiding-place. They trooped to the entrance of the cave and hung a magic mirror from the branches of a sakaki tree. Then they caused roosters to crow constantly, as if it were dawn.

A crowing rooster makes Amaterasu think that day has dawned

◀ *Izanami and Izanagi, page 26*

They lit bonfires, and, while some of the gods provided the music, a young goddess called Uzume climbed on to an upturned tub and began to dance. She shimmied and pranced – in a way that was at once so seductive and so funny that all eight million gods laughed and laughed until the heavens shook.

Amaterasu was so intrigued that she opened the cave door a crack and called, "What's going on?"

"We're celebrating," replied Uzume, "because we've found a goddess who shines even more brightly than you!"

Uzume's comic dancing lures Amaterasu out of the cave

Amaterasu

The gods bar the cave entrance and hang a mirror in a tree to make Amaterasu believe they have found a more radiant goddess

Amaterasu looked out, and the gods turned the magic mirror towards her, so that she saw her own reflection. As she gazed in wonder at her own radiant beauty, one of the gods seized her hand and pulled her from the cave, and another stretched a rope of straw across the entrance, saying, "This is as far as you may go."

So Amaterasu was tricked back into the world by the laughter of the gods and the beauty of her own reflection, and since that time the sun has never again failed.

As for Susanowo, the gods punished him for his part in the affair by cutting off his beard, and his fingernails and toenails, and banishing him from the High Plains of Heaven. But he and his powerful storms are still causing mischief on earth.

❖

SUSANOWO
There are many stories linked with Susanowo the storm god, some of which show him as good, some evil. In one, he rescues a goddess from being eaten by a dragon with eight heads. In another, his sister Amaterasu gives him jewels which he uses to make lightning and hail.

THE SWORD IN THE STONE

IT WAS CHRISTMAS. The squabbling barons and knights who had been fighting and feuding ever since the death of old King Uther Pendragon were gathered together in London's great church. They had been summoned by the enchanter Merlin, a wild figure who had been King Uther's chief advisor. No one knew why they were there.

When they came out of the church, they saw in the churchyard a mighty sword, sticking through a metal anvil into a huge block of marble. On the stone were the words: "Whoever pulls this sword from this stone is the rightful king of all England."

Every one of the barons and knights thought he should be king. They all tugged and wrenched at the sword, but none of them could budge it. At last, they all gave up.

It was announced that on New Year's Day, a tournament would be held. There would be jousting and feasting. Afterwards, anyone with a claim to the throne could try again to pull the sword from the stone.

People came from all over the country to take part in the tournament. Among them were a north-country knight, Sir Ector, and his sons: proud Sir Kay and his young brother Arthur.

*Not one of the knights or barons can
pull the sword from the stone*

Sir Kay   Sir Ector

Merlin

Kay was so excited about taking part in his first tournament that he forgot his sword. He did not realize his mistake until they had arrived at the jousting-field. "Go and fetch my sword from our lodgings," he told Arthur, "and look lively!"

Arthur rode as fast as he could back to the lodging house, but everyone was out and it was locked up. Kay had a nasty temper, and Arthur didn't want to have to tell him that he could not find his sword. So when he saw a sword sticking out of a stone in the churchyard, he decided to borrow it. He quickly pulled out the sword and took it with him.

As soon as Sir Kay saw the sword, he knew at once that it was the sword from the churchyard. He took it to Sir Ector, saying, "Father, look! I have pulled the sword from the stone. I must be the rightful king."

Sir Ector took Sir Kay and Arthur back to the churchyard. "Now," he said, "tell me again, Kay, how you got this sword."

Kay could not look his father in the eye. "Father, my brother Arthur brought it to me."

Then Sir Ector asked Arthur, "How did you come by this sword?"

"I hope I haven't done wrong," said Arthur. "Kay had forgotten his sword, and this one was sticking out of the stone. I only borrowed it. Let me put it back." And Arthur pushed the sword back through the anvil into the stone.

Sir Ector seized the hilt and pulled with all his strength. The sword resisted him. Then Sir Kay tried, and still the sword would not move. But when Arthur took hold of the sword, it answered to his hand and slid out of the stone like silk.

Sir Ector knelt down.

"Father, why are you kneeling?" asked Arthur.

The tournament gets under way on the jousting-field

Sir Ector and Sir Kay kneel before Arthur, the true king

JOUSTING

By the 13th century, jousting had become part of the tournament – a series of mock battles for entertainment. In a joust, two knights on horseback charged towards one another and tried to unseat each other with a wooden spear, called a lance.

Pommel

Crossguard

Fuller

KNIGHT'S SWORD

The sword was a knight's most prized weapon: a symbol of knighthood itself. This sword has a double cutting edge, and a groove, called a fuller, running down the centre of the blade to make it lighter.

NOBLE KING
Arthur ruled his kingdom with justice and honour, and his knights of the Round Table were expected to uphold these virtues. In this 13th-century carving, Arthur looks wise and thoughtful.

Merlin   Arthur   Guinevere

King Arthur's Round Table seats more than one hundred of the noblest knights that ever lived

THE ROUND TABLE
Arthur's table was round so that everyone who sat at it was of equal importance. The Winchester Table, above, dates from around 1300. It may have been made for the medieval pastime called Round Tables, at which nobles dressed up as Arthur's knights.

"I am not your father," confessed Sir Ector, "though I love you like a son. You were brought to my door one stormy night, a little squalling baby in the arms of Merlin, the wizard, the dream-reader. And now I understand that you must be the son of King Uther Pendragon, and the rightful king of all England."

And so it was that the boy Arthur, who was not even yet a knight, was acclaimed King of England by the people; for try as they might, no one else could ever shift the sword from the stone.

King Arthur, with Sir Kay at his right hand and Merlin at his left, set about bringing peace to the country. He married the beautiful Guinevere, and founded the order of the Knights of the Round Table. There were one hundred and fifty seats at that table, and whenever a knight was worthy to sit there, his name would appear, by Merlin's magic, on his seat.

Many famous knights came to sit at the Round Table in Camelot, including Sir Gawain, Sir Perceval, Sir Lancelot and Sir Galahad, the most perfect knight of them all. Their adventures in the cause of good will be told and retold forever, because these were the finest of all the noble knights who ever lived.

THE HOLY GRAIL

KING ARTHUR FILLED his Round Table with the best knights in all the world. But for many years, one seat remained empty. No one could sit on it and live, which is why it was called the Siege Perilous, or seat of danger. Merlin prophesied that when a knight came to claim the Siege Perilous, the days of the Round Table would be drawing to their close.

One day a young knight appeared at court, in red armour and without weapons. He bowed to King Arthur, walked straight to the Siege Perilous, and sat down. The knights gasped. But behind the young knight appeared in letters of gold, "Galahad, the High Prince".

"Welcome," said King Arthur. "Please tell us who you are."

"I am Sir Galahad, and my mother Elaine is the daughter of King Pelles, the Maimed King."

"I have heard of King Pelles, who lies crippled at the castle of Carbonek. But I did not know he had a grandson. And yet, Sir Galahad, I feel I know you. You look like Sir Lancelot as a young man."

"This is not surprising," said Lancelot, "for he is my son."

KNIGHTS ON A QUEST This 13th-century French manuscript illustration shows Galahad, Perceval, and Bors with the Holy Grail. These three knights went in search of the Grail, and were the only ones to find it.

Sir Galahad

The Siege Perilous

The Knights of the Round Table stare in amazement as the young knight walks straight to the Siege Perilous

The maiden lifts the cloth just enough to allow each knight to drink

THE ARDAGH CHALICE
The Holy Grail was thought to be a lost chalice, or cup, that contained Christ's blood. The sacred vessel may have been similar to this 8th-century Irish chalice from Ardagh.

That night, as the knights feasted, there was a tremendous storm outside. Thunder crashed overhead and lightning flooded the hall with light. The knights were silenced, and into that silence and strange light came a maiden bearing a vessel covered with a white cloth. And from that vessel each knight drank. And then the maiden left, and the unearthly light disappeared.

"What can this mean?" asked King Arthur.

Sir Galahad replied, "That vessel was the Holy Grail. I will not rest until I have seen it uncovered." The other knights agreed, "We must find the Grail, which has been lost for so long."

King Arthur was reluctant to let them go, for he foresaw that this was no ordinary quest, and that many of his knights must fail, and perhaps die along the way. He knew now why Merlin had told him that the day the Siege Perilous was filled would be the day that the Fellowship of the Round Table would begin to crumble. But once the knights had sworn to search for the Grail, they had to do so.

King Arthur's knights set out in all directions, each following his own way. Their adventures on this, the greatest of all quests, would easily fill a book on their own. But most of these tales tell of knights who lost their way and became embroiled in fights and love affairs. The quest for the Holy Grail was not for worldly men such as these, but only for the pure in heart.

Of all the knights of the Round Table, three rode together, free from rivalry, greed, or ambition, searching for the Grail with all their hearts and minds. They were Sir Perceval, Sir Bors, and Sir Galahad. And behind them rode Sir Lancelot, begging God's forgiveness for falling in love with Guinevere, Arthur's queen.

Sir Perceval, Sir Bors, and Sir Galahad arrived at a seashore and found a magic ship waiting for them. They stepped on board, and at once the ship set sail. It took them to the castle of Carbonek, where Sir Galahad's grandfather, King Pelles, ruled over a blighted kingdom from his bed of pain.

In King Pelles's bedchamber, the strange, intense light appeared again. Two maidens appeared. The first was carrying the Holy Grail, as before, but this time it was uncovered, and it was clear that it was the source of the light. The other maiden carried a spear that seemed to weep blood from its tip in great drops, which the first maiden caught in the Grail.

"What does this mean?" asked Sir Galahad.

"The spear is the weapon that pierced Our Lord's side as He hung on the Cross. The vessel is the Holy Grail, in which were caught the drops of His blood that fell from the wound."

Sir Galahad took the spear and touched King Pelles with its tip. At once the King was made well again, and his blighted kingdom began to bloom once more. Then they all went into the chapel and celebrated Mass, but this time only Sir Galahad saw the Holy Grail uncovered, for he alone of all the Knights of the Round Table was utterly pure in thought and deed. When he had done so, he seemed to

❖

THE CRUSADES
The Grail myth may have been inspired by the Crusades, holy wars fought in the Middle East (then known as the Holy Land) between Christians and Muslims. Unlike Arthur's knights, however, the Christian Crusaders were more interested in power and plunder than religion.

Sir Galahad | Sir Perceval | King Pelles | Sir Bors

Sir Galahad touches King Pelles with the spear, making him well again and bringing renewed life to his kingdom

fill with light, until he became one with it. Then he, the maidens, the spear, and the Grail itself disappeared from the world of men for ever.

Sir Bors and Sir Perceval came out of the chapel and found Sir Lancelot lying exhausted on the ground. Strength of will had carried him thus far, but, despite repenting all his sins, he was not worthy to enter the chapel and see the Grail uncovered – even though he was the greatest knight who ever bore arms.

❖

SIR LANCELOT
Lancelot was the most splendid of Arthur's knights, but his chivalrous reputation was ruined by his love affair with Queen Guinevere. Because of this, Lancelot was not able to see the Grail.

The Death of King Arthur, page 156 ➤

GLOOSKAP AND THE WASIS

GOLDEN HOMELAND
Many of the Algonquin tribes are from the densely wooded northeast of North America. This may help to explain their belief that when Glooskap fired arrows at some birch trees, the first people appeared from their bark. Birch bark was used for canoe building and for making bowls and other utensils. It is a sacred material for some tribes.

❖

A GOD SAILS AWAY
Glooskap taught mankind many things, but at last lost patience with people's sinfulness and ingratitude. He sailed away in a canoe, but one day he will return to save his people from evil.

GLOOSKAP WAS THE MIGHTIEST WARRIOR of all. He was the Lord of Men and Beasts. He had mastered the ghosts of the night and the spirits of the day. At last, having achieved many great feats during his wanderings, Glooskap decided to return home. But when he entered his house, his wife barely gave him so much as a glance.

She was looking at a creature on the floor. Glooskap had battled ghosts, and devils, and wild animals of every kind, but he had never seen anything like it.

"What is it?" he asked.

"It is the mighty Wasis," she replied. "And I warn you, if you meddle with him, you will be in trouble. I must serve him night and day."

"I wouldn't put up with such a tyrant," said Glooskap.

"You would have no choice," said the woman. "The mighty Wasis holds the past in one hand, and the future in the other. He is master of all the world."

"Not of me," cried Glooskap. "I am Lord of Men and Beasts. Nothing can defeat me!"

He walked right up to the mighty Wasis.

"I am not afraid of you," he said.

The Wasis gurgled.

Glooskap took up his fighting stance. "I am the strongest," he said.

The Wasis sat and sucked on some maple-sugar.

"I am Lord of Men and Beasts," thundered Glooskap. "Come here!"

But the Wasis howled back. He screamed and screamed and screamed until Glooskap thought his head would split.

Having mastered wild beasts and ghostly spirits, Glooskap returns home

"Stop that!" he shouted.

But the mighty Wasis just kept on screaming.

Desperate to quiet him, Glooskap danced his ghost dance and sang the songs that raise the dead.

Then Glooskap danced his spirit dance and sang the songs that scare away devils.

And, at long last, the Wasis stopped screaming, looked at Glooskap, and smiled, a big smile as wide as the world. "Goo!" he said.

Totally exhausted by his heroic efforts to stop the Wasis screaming and howling, Glooskap collapsed in a dead faint.

So whenever you see a baby sitting on the floor with a big smile all over its face, chuckling "Goo! Goo!" for no reason at all, you may be sure it is remembering the day it defeated the great Glooskap, the Lord of Men and Beasts, who had conquered the whole wide world.

MEDICINE BAG
Among the tribes of northeastern America, bags such as this are used to hold medicinal charms and herbs. They are made of otterskin (the otter symbolizes healing power). At one time, when a healer died, his bag was often buried with him. However medicine bags now tend to be passed on from father to son or otherwise kept within the tribe.

For of all the beings that have ever been created since the Beginning, a baby is the only one that nobody has ever got the better of – nor ever will, until the End of Time.

Despite all Glooskap's strength, he is no match for the mighty Wasis and its terrible bellowing

TELEPINU

THE HITTITES
The ancient people
from whose mythology
this story comes
established a powerful
empire in Anatolia (in
modern-day Turkey)
around 1590 BC. The
Hittite Empire collapsed
in about 1200 BC, but
aspects of the Hittite
civilization lived on for
several centuries in
parts of Anatolia and
what is now Syria.

THE WEATHER GOD
This relief shows the
Hittite weather god
wearing distinctive
Hittite clothing – a
pointed hat and a short
tunic tied with a sash.
In the Hittite family of
gods, the weather god
was important, but not
as powerful as the
mother goddess.

TELEPINU, GOD OF FARMING, grew angry with the world; no one knows why. He was in such a rage that, in his haste to depart, he put his left boot on his right foot and his right boot on his left foot.

Without him, the world grew covered with mist. Logs in the fire refused to burn; the gods could not hear the prayers of men. Both men and gods began to starve.

The weather god hammers on his son Telepinu's door

Angry with the world, Telepinu, god of farming, pulls on his boots

Telepinu's father, the weather god, grew worried. Hannahanna, the mother goddess, implored him to find his son before everything died.

They sent out an eagle to search for Telepinu, but it could not find him. Then the weather god himself went to Telepinu's house and battered on the gates with his hammer, but to no avail.

So Hannahanna said, "Let us send a bee to look for him."

"Don't be ridiculous," said the weather god. "A bee is too small to be of any use." But Hannahanna sent it anyway.

"Let us send a bee to look for Telepinu," says Hannahanna, the mother goddess

The bee searched far and wide, and eventually found the god asleep in the wilderness. As Hannahanna had instructed it, the bee stung Telepinu on the hands and on the feet, and smeared wax on Telepinu's eyes.

At last the bee finds Telepinu

Hannahanna thought this would bring Telepinu to his senses; but it only made him angrier still. His renewed rage caused floods to rise, and houses, men, and animals were swept away.

At last Kamrusepas, the goddess of healing and magic, was called. She stood on a mountainside, with twelve rams as a sacrifice to appease Telepinu's anger.

Kamrusepas cried, "Doorkeeper of the Underworld, open the seven doors, unlock the seven bolts. Into your cauldrons of bronze, receive Telepinu's rage, his malice, his fury. Let them not come back!"

Telepinu returns on the back of an eagle

Kamrusepas, goddess of magic, asks the Doorkeeper to receive Telepinu's anger

A ram's fleece, corn, wine, and oxen are offered to Telepinu on his return

Then, with a loud roll of thunder, and streams of lightning, Telepinu returned, riding on the back of an eagle.

The people set up a pole before him, hung with the fleece of a ram, and placed offerings of corn, wine, and oxen around its base.

Telepinu was pleased with these things, for they spoke to him of growth, and plenty, of long life and children. His anger was gone.

TELEPINU
The myth of Telepinu has parallels in other cultures. When the god of agriculture disappears, the earth dies; when he returns, everything begins to grow again.

HATTUSHASH
The imposing ruins of the ancient Hittite capital city of Hattushash (present day Bogazköy in Turkey) are still guarded by the massive stone lions of the Western Gate (above). Hattushash was a thriving city from about 1650 to 1200 BC, owing mainly to the Hittites' military strength and to their silver and iron mines, which were the richest in Asia Minor. When Hattushash was excavated, over 10,000 cuneiform tablets, containing myths – such as this tale of Telepinu – literature, and historical records of the Hittites were found.

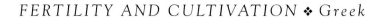

CADMUS AND THE SOWN MEN

ATHENA
The goddess Athena, depicted on this coin from the 5th century BC, was a warrior and favourite daughter of Zeus. She was known for her good sense, and is associated with the owl, an ancient symbol of wisdom. Athena was also the patron goddess of Athens.

WARRIOR
This detail from the "Warrior Vase" shows a Greek soldier carrying a shield and a spear. The vase, which comes from Mycenae in southern Greece, can be dated to c.1200 BC.

C ADMUS HAD A SISTER named Europa. She was carried off by Zeus, who was disguised as a bull, and became the mother of King Minos of Crete. When Europa disappeared, Cadmus went in search of her. For many months he scoured the lands around his home, but could find no sign of his sister. At last he went to Delphi to consult the oracle, where the advice and prophecies of the god Apollo were revealed. Cadmus asked the oracle what he should do.

"Your sister is safe. Search for her no more," said the oracle. "Your destiny lies elsewhere. When you leave here, you will see a cow. Follow it, and when it falls to the ground, exhausted, there you must build a great city."

Outside Delphi, Cadmus saw a cow, just as the oracle had promised. With a group of men he followed it for many miles until at last it sank to the ground. "Here we will found our city, and call it Thebes," said Cadmus. "But first, we must sacrifice this cow to the goddess Athena. Go and fetch some water from the spring to honour the goddess."

The oracle of Apollo tells Cadmus that a cow will show him where to build a new city

Cadmus sees the cow and follows it

◄ *Persephone, page 82*

When the men took water from the spring, they disturbed a terrible serpent, which killed them all with its fearsome, snapping jaws. In fury, Cadmus slew the serpent with a blow from a huge rock.

No sooner had Cadmus sacrificed the cow than the goddess Athena appeared. She told him not to worry about the loss of his men. "I will supply you with better men than any king can command. Just take the serpent's teeth and sow them in the soil."

❖

THE FIRST THEBANS
The "sown men" were known as the *spartoi*, from the Greek "to sow". The five who survived were the first inhabitants of the city of Thebes, of which Cadmus was king.

When Cadmus sows the serpent's teeth, an army of warriors bursts from the earth

Cadmus did as he was told, and from the soil sprang fully grown men, warriors all. Before the men could turn on him, Cadmus threw a stone amongst them, and they fought so fiercely about who had thrown it that in the end only five survived. Cadmus made peace with them, and these warriors, the strongest and the fiercest of all the sown men, helped him establish the great city of Thebes.

Theseus and the Minotaur, page 108 ➤

MOTHER OF LIFE AND DEATH

MOTHER OF DEATH
This relief from the 8th century AD shows the goddess Durga killing the demon Mahisha who has taken on the form of a giant water buffalo.

THE GODDESS DEVI is the consort of Shiva, god of generation and destruction. She is the mother of all, holding in her hands both joy and pain, life and death. She is known under many names, in many forms.

As mother of life, Devi brings the rain and protects against disease. She is mild and loving.

As mother of death, she is terrible.

As Durga, the yellow-haired warrior goddess, she is frightening enough. She has eight arms, and rides into battle against her foes.

Devi holds life and death in her hands

But when Durga is enraged, the goddess Kali springs from her forehead, and then it is not only the wicked who must cower in fear, but the good also. For Kali is so deadly and furious a fighter that she becomes entirely consumed with bloodlust. If she is not stopped, she will rampage through the world, fighting until no one is left alive.

Durga herself is a fighter almost without equal. She came into being to protect the gods against the demon Mahisha, who, in the form of a huge water buffalo, had been terrorizing them with its deadly hooves and horns, and with the hurricane of its breath. Neither Vishnu, the protector, nor, Shiva, the destroyer, could defeat it.

❖

THE GODDESS DEVI
Devi, whose name means "goddess", is the Divine Mother of the Hindu religion. She has many forms. As well as the warlike Durga and the terrifying Kali, who both appear in this story, she can be gentle, as the beautiful Parvati and the religious Uma.

Durga

The warrior goddess Durga attacks the demon Mahisha

Mahisha

Durga rode against the buffalo on her lion and caught it in a noose. Then Mahisha changed himself into a lion. Durga cut off the lion's head, but the demon became a man armed with a sword and shield. Durga shot the man with an arrow, and Mahisha turned into a huge elephant, trumpeting defiance. Durga cut off the elephant's trunk with her sword, and Mahisha turned once more into a monstrous buffalo. The buffalo charged at her, but she leapt first, red-eyed and laughing in her battle-fury.

She mounted the buffalo and kicked it in the neck. As she did so, Mahisha's spirit was driven half out of the buffalo's mouth. Durga swung her sword and cut off the demon's head. When the buffalo fell, all the gods cried, "Victory!" All the demons wailed in anguish.

Once, however, Durga was hard pressed in battle with the demon lords Chanda and Munda, and the demon Raktabija. The reason was this: every time a drop of Raktabija's blood touched the ground, a replica of the demon instantly arose. The harder Durga fought against him, the more replicas of him there were to fight.

So Durga summoned Kali, and she came. Her tongue lolled from her fanged mouth to savour the blood in the air. In one of her four hands she held a bloodstained sword.

First, with a roar, she slew the demon lords. Then she attacked Raktabija himself, swiping off his head with one stroke of her sword. Her tongue shot out and caught his blood as it fell, and then she drained his body dry. The few little demons that sprang up where droplets of the demon's blood touched the ground, she swallowed whole.

Such is the wrath of Devi, the mother, who holds the universe in her womb.

DEVI AS KALI
This 18th-century painting shows Kali, the most bloodthirsty form of the goddess Devi, whose long tongue laps blood. In her left hands she holds tokens of death – a sword, and a severed head. However in one right hand she carries a holy book, and with the other she blesses her followers. The Indian city of Calcutta is named after the goddess Kali.

❖

SHIVA
Shiva, an important Hindu god, has a third eye that flashes fire in the middle of his forehead. He was roused from life as a religious hermit by an arrow of desire fired by Kama the god of love. This caused Shiva to fall in love with a beautiful mountain girl, Parvati, one of the forms of the goddess Devi. Shiva is both terrifying and gentle, destructive and merciful.

Kali beheads Raktabija

Kali

Raktabija's head

Demons spring from Raktabija's blood

The Elephant God, page 144 ➤

GODS AND MORTALS

While creator gods may choose to leave the world once their work is done, other gods and goddesses find men and women endlessly fascinating.

Not content with merely looking on, these immortals cannot resist meddling directly in the lives of human beings, leading to all kinds of extraordinary adventures and happenings. Some gods even fall in love with mortals, and from such unions come many of the heroes of mythology. These semi-divine beings possess remarkable qualities, usually great strength or cunning. Sometimes a gift from the gods may come by accident, as in the tale of Taliesin, an ordinary boy who is transformed into Wales's greatest poet. And sometimes, as King Midas discovers, a gift from an immortal may turn out to be a terrible curse, not a blessing.

Hugi the giant outruns Thialfi in Thor in the Land of Giants, *in which giants hoodwink gods and men alike*

THE GOLDEN TOUCH

❖

SATYRS
The satyrs were woodland gods; often the lower parts of their bodies resembled horses or goats. Silenus was older but, like the other satyrs, was a companion of Dionysus.

THE GIFTS OF THE gods are not always what they seem. Take warning from the tale of King Midas, who thought himself wise. Midas had been tutored in the mysteries of the god of wine, Dionysus, by the poet Orpheus. So when one day some peasants brought before him an old, drunken satyr, bound with chains of flowers, Midas recognized him as Silenus, a companion of Dionysus.

Midas feasted Silenus for ten days and nights and, in return, Silenus told him many strange things. He told of a terrible whirlpool beyond which no traveller may pass. Beside it, two streams flow. By the first grows a tree whose fruit causes those who eat it to waste away. By the second grows a tree whose fruit will make men young again. One bite takes an old man back to middle age; two bites and he is a young man again; in three bites he is back in adolescence; in four he is a child; in five, a baby. Take a sixth bite, and he will disappear altogether.

At length, Midas took Silenus back to Dionysus, by the banks of the River Pactolus. The god had been missing his companion, and by way of gratitude for Silenus's safe return, he offered to grant Midas any wish he might ask for.

Midas first thought of Silenus's tale, but then he remembered a story that when he was a baby, some ants had been seen carrying golden grains of wheat and placing them between his lips – a sign of great wealth to come. So, instead of choosing youth, Midas said, "Grant that whatever I touch will turn to gold."

The fat satyr, Silenus, tells Midas some strange tales as he drinks his wine

GOLDEN TREASURE
This jug with coins, dating from 650-625 BC, was found in Ephesus, Turkey. The coins are made of electrum, an alloy of gold and silver used in ancient times.

As a baby, Midas is fed by ants on golden grains of wheat

The god granted Midas's wish, and the king went away, delighted with his good fortune. He broke a twig from a low-growing branch of oak, and it turned to gold. He touched a stone and a clod of earth, and they, too, turned to gold. He gathered an ear of corn and it turned to glittering metal in his hand. He picked an apple, and it became as golden as the fabled apples of the Hesperides.

He touched the pillars of his palace doorway, and they turned to gold. Even the water in which he washed splashed golden over his hands. He called for food and wine. But when he reached for a piece of bread, it too turned to gold; when he bit into some meat, it turned to metal where his teeth touched it. Even the wine, Dionysus's discovery and gift to men, turned to liquid gold as it passed his lips.

Midas could neither eat nor drink, and soon he was in a torment of hunger and thirst. Gold, which had once been his heart's desire, was now hateful to him. He begged Dionysus to free him from his gift.

Dionysus took pity on the wretched man, and told him, "To cancel the gift, you must go to the source of the River Pactolus. Bathe in the spring there, and wash away your greed." Midas did as he was told and, as he bathed, his golden touch washed away into the river. The waters ran with gold, and even now the soil along the riverbank has a golden gleam.

WINE VESSELS
In Ancient Greece wine was a popular drink. It was believed to be the gift of the god Dionysus to mankind. Wine was often diluted, and the larger of these two bronze wine vessels would have held water for this purpose. The mixture was poured into a jug and the ladle used to fill the cups.

Midas washes away his golden touch in the river

Everything Midas touches turns to gold, including his food and wine

King Midas's Ears, page 104 ➤

KING MIDAS'S EARS

APOLLO
This statue of Apollo, with a smile on his face, dates from 575-550 BC. Apollo, who was the god of music and light, had beautiful long, curling hair.

THERE IS ANOTHER STORY of Midas, which shows that although he freed himself from the desire for gold, he did not rid himself of foolishness. For he became a worshipper of Pan, the god of pastures and wild places and, by taking Pan's side, he offended great Apollo.

Now Pan enjoys playing simple country tunes on his wooden pipes, and because everyone always likes what they hear, he began to boast that he was a better musician even than Apollo, the god of music. He went so far as to challenge Apollo to a contest, to be judged by the river god Tmolus.

Tmolus dressed himself as a judge, with an oak wreath in his hair and bunches of acorns hanging by his brow, and sat down to listen to the music. Pan played first, and his merry piping charmed everyone. But then Apollo took up his lyre, and the notes he plucked rippled on the breeze like waves across the ocean, liquid and delicious.

Tmolus and Midas judge the music contest between Pan and Apollo

Pan

Midas

Tmolus

Apollo

Midas is horrified to find that he has ass's ears

DONKEY CUP
The painted pottery of ancient Greece often features figures and scenes from Greek mythology. Less common are the cups and jugs shaped as animals. This unusual two-handled drinking cup has a donkey's head as a spout for pouring.

❖

THE PAN PIPES
King Midas is said to have invented the pipes that Pan played in the music contest. This is perhaps why he preferred Pan's playing to Apollo's.

Tmolus had no hesitation in awarding the prize to Apollo, but Midas objected. "I preferred Pan's playing," he said.

"You can't have heard properly," said Tmolus.

"There's nothing wrong with my ears," said Midas.

At that, Apollo's anger overflowed. "You are not fit to have human ears," he said, "if that is the use you make of them." And he gave Midas, instead, a pair of ass's ears: long, grey, and hairy. "Now you look the donkey you are," he said.

King Midas was ashamed of his new ears, and tried to hide them from the world by wrapping them up in a turban. However his barber eventually discovered his embarrassing secret.

The barber did not dare tell anyone about the king's strange deformity, but he could not keep such an extraordinary thing to himself. So he went out into the country, dug a hole, and whispered the secret into the ground. Then he buried it underneath the earth.

But all secrets will out. A clump of reeds grew where the barber had dug his hole, and as the wind whistled through them, they sighed, and seemed to call, "King Midas has ass's ears! King Midas has ass's ears!"

When he learned that his secret was common knowledge, Midas died of shame.

Everyone hears the reeds whisper, "King Midas has ass's ears"

The Death of Pan, page 172 ➤

BEOWULF

❖

EPIC POEM
The poem of Beowulf
was sung or recited long
before it was written
down. The version we
know today originated
in the 8th century,
though the only
surviving manuscript
dates from the 10th.

HROTHGAR, KING OF THE Danes, built a great feasting hall at Heorot. There he gave arm rings of gold and other gifts to reward his followers; there mead was drunk, boasts were made and bards sang of all the wonders of the world. The sound of merrymaking rang from the rafters.

Outside, lurking in the brackish fens, was an evil creature, Grendel by name – a vile monster that stalked the borderlands. The sound of bright laughter caused it pain. Night after night it endured the torment. Then, driven beyond endurance, it ventured to Heorot. The men in the hall were slumbering, their heads full of ale and their bellies full of food. Grendel broke their necks and dragged them off like slaughtered meat to its lair.

The monstrous Grendel drags a victim to his lair in the fens

❖

THE ANGLO-SAXONS
After the Romans left
Britain, around AD 400,
the Britons asked north
European tribes – the
Angles, Saxons, Jutes,
and Frisians – to help
them fight the Picts and
Scots. These "Anglo-
Saxons" defeated the
Britons' enemies, but
then began waging war
on the Britons. By AD
600 they had conquered
large parts of Britain.

Grendel visited Hrothgar's hall each night for twelve years. In all that time, no songs or laughter were heard there. But at last a hero came, Beowulf of the Geats, who declared, "I will kill this monster, or die."

"No one can stand against it," jeered Unferth, one of Hrothgar's men, "still less a lad like you."

Beowulf vows to kill the monster with his bare hands

"I will kill it with my bare hands," replied Beowulf.

That night Grendel broke into the hall once more. Beowulf seized the monster and wrestled with it. And with a horrible, wet, tearing sound, he pulled its mighty arm clean from its body. The monster howled and, moaning pitifully, fled into the dark.

The next night, all rejoiced. But they celebrated too soon. For in the dark, an even viler creature came, and killed Aeschere, the king's

great friend. It was Grendel's mother, come to avenge her offspring.

Beowulf tracked her across the moors to the lake where she lurked.

"I am sorry for what I said," said Unferth. "Here, take my sword, Hrunting. It never fails."

Beowulf dived into the lake. Down and down he swam, till he reached the monster's lair. She clawed at him, but his corslet of metal rings protected him. He swung at her, but Unferth's sword could not pierce her tough hide. Then he saw, lying on the bottom, a great sword, made for a giant. Beowulf alone of mortal men could have lifted it. He seized it, and struck.

The waters of the lake boiled with blood.

The men watching ashore said, "Beowulf is dead." But suddenly he surfaced, holding the heads of both Grendel and Grendel's mother.

LAND OF MONSTERS
The Anglo-Saxons did not find it hard to believe that hideous monsters lurked in the mists, marshes, and stagnant pools of fenlands, such as these in Cambridgeshire, England.

The young warrior seizes the great sword from the bottom of the lake and strikes at Grendel's mother

WINGED DRAGON
This bronze, winged dragon, part of the decoration on an Anglo-Saxon chief's shield, is just one of the many treasures that were found in the burial ship at Sutton Hoo, Suffolk, England, in the late 1930s.

Then there was feasting and giving of gifts, until Beowulf and his men took ship once more on the gull's path, the whale's way, back to the land of the Geats, where Beowulf was to be king.

THESEUS AND THE MINOTAUR

MOUNTAINOUS CRETE
The Greek island of Crete is a place of contrasts: snow-capped mountains as well as fertile valleys. Between 2500 and 1100 BC, Crete was occupied by the Minoans, named after the legendary King Minos.

GREAT ZEUS HAS HAD many human lovers, whom he attracts using different disguises. Many of these lovers have borne him children upon whose fates the whole world has turned. One such lover was Europa, whom Zeus saw walking by the shore. He disguised himself as a snow-white bull and approached her. Amazed at seeing a bull at once so fine and so tame, Europa petted him and hung flowers from his horns. Then, suddenly bold, she jumped on to his back and let him carry her down to the sea.

Once in the water, Zeus swam away with Europa across the ocean to the island of Crete, where, disguised as an eagle, he lay with her. She bore him three sons: Minos, Rhadamanthys, and Sarpedon.

After Zeus left her, Europa married Asterius, King of Crete, who raised her sons as his own, making Minos his heir. In due course Minos became king and took the lovely Pasiphae for his wife. In his pride and glory, Minos boasted that the gods themselves would grant his requests. To prove it, he built an altar to Poseidon on the seashore and prayed that a wonderful bull should come to him out of the sea. Minos promised he would then sacrifice the bull to the gods.

Immediately, a white bull emerged from the waves. But it was such a fine beast that Minos could not bear to sacrifice it; instead, he killed a bull from his own herd, and kept the gift of the gods for himself. For this insolence, the gods took a terrible revenge.

Aphrodite, goddess of love, made Minos's wife, Pasiphae, fall in love with the bull. Horrified, but unable to resist Aphrodite's power, Pasiphae confided her secret to Daedalus, a great craftsman who served King Minos and his court at Knossos.

So Daedalus built a hollow, wooden cow for Pasiphae to crouch inside. From there, unseen, she was able to spend time with the bull, her beloved. But as further punishment, the gods caused Pasiphae to give birth to a monster, half-man, half-bull, that was named the Minotaur.

Pasiphae crouches inside the wooden cow that Daedalus has made for her and waits for the white bull to approach

◀ *Cadmus and the Sown Men, page 96*

Minos was filled with horror at what had happened to Pasiphae, and sought advice from an oracle. "Conceal your shame in cunning," he was told. So Minos asked Daedalus to build the Labyrinth, a maze of winding passages with sudden twists and turns and dead ends, through which no man could find his way. At the centre of the maze he put the Minotaur. To feed this monster,

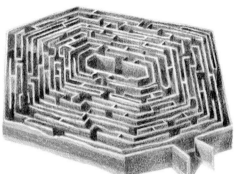

The Minotaur was imprisoned in the middle of Daedalus's Labyrinth

Every nine years, seven young men and seven maidens are sacrificed to the Minotaur

King Minos demanded seven young men and seven maidens from the city of Athens every nine years. They were sent by ship to Crete and then into the maze, where the Minotaur glutted himself on their flesh.

Twice Athens had paid this deadly tribute, owed by the king, Aegeus, because some years before he had had an accidental hand in the death of Minos's son. The third time was now due. But on this occasion a young hero stepped forward, offering himself as one of the youths, and promising to kill the Minotaur or be killed by it. His name was Theseus, the adopted son of King Aegeus, whose real father was the sea-god Poseidon. Theseus had already proved himself resourceful and brave and Aegeus had to let him go. He told Theseus, "Before, the ships I sent to Crete bore black sails, in mourning for the young people who were to be killed by the Minotaur. This time, the ship will also carry white sails, in token of our hope. If you slay the beast, be sure to hoist the white sails on your return, so we will know that you have been successful, and can rejoice." With that, the ship set sail.

MINOTAUR COIN
This 400-BC coin was found at Knossos in Crete. The palace of Knossos, with its many winding corridors, may have inspired the myth of the Labyrinth.

When the ship landed at Crete, Theseus at once sprang to shore and, announcing himself as the son of Poseidon, challenged Minos.

"Son of Poseidon!" sneered Minos. "Great Zeus will bear witness that I am his son, but will Poseidon own up to you?"

Theseus dived headlong into the sea, where a school of dolphins, arching their backs above the foam, escorted him all the way down to the seabed. There he

A school of dolphins escorts Theseus to the depths of the ocean, where Amphitrite gives him a ring and a crown as a sign of favour

received from Amphitrite, goddess of the sea, a golden ring and a jewelled crown. When the dolphins brought him back to shore, he held up the precious gifts, so that all could see the favour he had found with the gods.

"Now, King Minos," he declared, "I have come to free the Minotaur from the misshapen body in which it has been trapped by the malice of the gods and the foolishness of mankind. If you are anything of a man, you will allow me to enter the Labyrinth and kill the creature, with my bare hands. If I succeed, Athens will owe you no more tribute. If I fail, let the Minotaur drink my blood."

"Very well," said King Minos. "You may try, son of Poseidon."

The next day, King Minos's daughter, Ariadne, who had fallen in love with the noble Theseus, approached him, saying, "If you will take me back to Athens and make me your bride, I will show you the key to the maze, given to me by Daedalus, its architect."

DOLPHIN OIL CONTAINER
The ancient Greeks gave special power to dolphins, which often appear in their art. This dolphin pitcher would have held cooking oil.

Theseus readily agreed, and Ariadne handed him a ball of thread.

"Tie one end of this thread outside the entrance of the maze," she said. "Then let the ball roll where it will. Follow it, and it will lead you to the centre, where you will find the foul lair of my half-brother, the Minotaur. Go at night, when he is asleep, and you may throttle him where he lies. Afterwards, simply roll the ball back up again, and it will lead you safely out."

That night, Theseus did as Ariadne instructed. As he plunged into the dark warren of the maze, the thread seemed to glimmer and guide his footsteps towards his prey.

As Theseus laid hands on the sleeping beast, it awoke and, with a roar, seized him in its death embrace. But Theseus was the stronger, and as they wrestled, he broke the creature's back and killed it.

Ariadne waits anxiously at the door as Theseus wrestles with the Minotaur

When Theseus staggered out of the maze, his face a mask of white and his body spotted with blood, Ariadne was there to meet him. They boarded their ship, with the other Athenian youths, and fled before King Minos could learn what had happened.

But Theseus was not true to Ariadne. She had helped him out of love, and he had accepted her help knowing he did not truly want to marry her. When, a few days later, they landed on the island of Naxos, Theseus left Ariadne sleeping on the shore and set sail without her.

So taken up was Theseus with his desertion of Ariadne, that he forgot all about the promise that he had made to his father. And so, when his ship came within sight of Athens, it bore still the black sails of mourning, not the white sails of victory. King Aegeus, who loved Theseus more than life, cast himself into the sea, which ever since his death, has been called the Aegean.

Thus the heroism of Theseus was tainted by treachery, and his joyful homecoming darkened by grief.

❖

THESEUS
Aegeus's adopted son Theseus was one of the greatest Greek heroes. After killing the Minotaur and Aegeus's tragic death, he became King of Athens. He later lived the life of a wandering adventurer.

Theseus's ship returns with black sails

The Fall of Icarus, page 112 ➤

THE FALL OF ICARUS

O F ALL THE CRAFTSMEN and inventors of old, Daedalus was the best and most famous. Anyone who wanted any clever thing made came first to him, at his workshop in Athens.

Now Daedalus had a nephew, Talos, who was the son of his sister, Polycaste. He took on Talos as his apprentice, and the boy, although only twelve years old, rapidly showed signs of being even cleverer than his master! It was Talos who invented the first saw and the potter's wheel, and Talos who devised the first pair of compasses. Talos's reputation soon spread and people began to bring their most difficult problems to the boy, not the man.

GREEK POTTERY
Most towns in ancient Greece had an area where potters made and sold pots. The wine cup above, made c. 490 BC, shows a potter at his wheel, adding a handle to a cup. The cup painter was usually a different person from the potter. Painted scenes such as these tell us about the everyday life and mythology of ancient Greece.

❖

MASTER CRAFTSMAN
Daedalus, the father of Icarus, was well known in Athens for his skill as an artist and craftsman. When jealousy caused him to murder his nephew Talos, he took refuge with King Minos on the island of Crete. There he became the architect of the Labyrinth, the maze that housed the monstrous Minotaur.

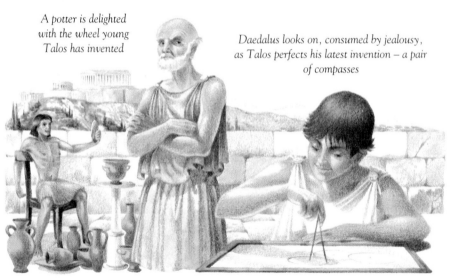

A potter is delighted with the wheel young Talos has invented

Daedalus looks on, consumed by jealousy, as Talos perfects his latest invention – a pair of compasses

Overcome with jealousy, Daedalus lured the boy to the top of the temple of Athena and then pushed him to his death. Talos's mother, Polycaste, killed herself out of grief, and Daedalus, along with his own son, Icarus – a vain boy with none of Talos's quickness – was banished from the city of Athens.

Daedalus and Icarus took refuge on the island of Crete, where Daedalus placed his skill and cleverness at the disposal of King Minos. But he suddenly fell out of favour with the king when Theseus killed the Minotaur and managed to escape from the supposedly escape-proof Labyrinth Daedalus had built to house the creature. Furious, King Minos had Deadalus and his son thrown into prison.

◄ *Theseus and the Minotaur, page 108*

While Icarus spent his days preening himself and thinking idle thoughts, Daedalus sat in deep study, planning how to escape from Crete. It was too far to swim to the nearest land, and impossible to get away by boat, owing to the vigilance of King Minos's navy.

At last Daedalus conceived a daring plan. He made two pairs of wings, threading feathers together and sealing them with wax. When the wings were ready, he took Icarus aside. "Put these on and follow me," he said, "but take care not to fly too near the sun, or too near the sea. Keep a middle course. With these wings, we shall escape."

The pair took flight from a high ledge and swooped towards the horizon. For many miles young Icarus followed his father carefully, but at last, feeling young and carefree, and enjoying the buffeting of the wind, he began to soar upwards into the sky, free as a bird.

THE ISLAND OF SAMOS
It is said that when Icarus flew too close to the sun and melted his wings, he fell into the sea near the Greek island of Samos.

When Icarus flies too close to the sun, the wax binding his wings melts and he tumbles to his doom

When Daedalus looked around for him, he was nowhere to be seen.

"Icarus! Icarus!" called the anxious father. But no reply came. Only, in the water far below, a scatter of feathers bobbed on the waves, and a few faint ripples spread from the spot where Icarus had fallen to his doom. For the boy had flown too near the sun, and the wax binding his wings had melted like butter.

Aeneas in the Underworld, page 154 ➤

TALIESIN

THE WITCH CERIDWEN had a daughter, Creiwry, who was the most beautiful girl in the world, and a son, Avagddu, who was the ugliest boy. Because Avagddu was so ugly, Ceridwen resolved to brew a cauldron of Inspiration and Knowledge for him. Once he had tasted it, he would know all the secrets of the future, and men would honour him for his wisdom, not spurn him for his ugliness.

She mixed the magic potion and set the cauldron boiling. It had to boil for a year and a day, and at the end of that time, it would yield just three precious drops of Inspiration and Knowledge.

She set a blind man named Morda to kindle the fire beneath the cauldron, and a boy named Gwion to stir it, and she herself gathered the special herbs that had to be added to the mixture each day.

But on the very last day, as Ceridwen was adding the final herbs, three drops splashed up from the cauldron on to Gwion's finger. The drops scalded him, and he put his finger in his mouth to ease the pain. At once he saw all that was, and is, and will be. Gwion fled.

SNOWDONIA, WALES
The tale of Taliesin unfolds against the wild, mountainous landscape of north Wales.

The witch Ceridwen brews a cauldron of Inspiration and Knowledge for her son, Avagddu

The boy Gwion licks three drops of the witch's brew from his finger

Ceridwen becomes a greyhound in order to pursue Gwion

Behind him, the cauldron cracked, and Ceridwen let out a curse. The witch set after Gwion. He saw her coming and changed into a hare, but she changed into a greyhound to chase him. He leapt into the river and became a fish, and she became an otter to catch him. He changed into a bird, and she became a hawk above him.

He dived into a pile of wheat and changed into a golden grain. Ceridwen turned into a black hen, and swallowed him whole.

Nine months she carried him, until at last he was born again. He was so beautiful that she could not bear to kill him, but cast him upon the sea, wrapped in a leather bag, to live or die.

Elphin

Ceridwen

Prince Elphin rescues the baby and calls him Taliesin

Each time Gwion changes into an animal to escape Ceridwen, she turns into a more cunning creature to catch him

The baby was found by a prince named Elphin, who rescued him from the water. Elphin called him Taliesin, which means "radiant brow", because of his beauty. Taliesin became Elphin's bard, or court poet and, because he had tasted the three drops of Inspiration and Knowledge, he soon became the greatest poet in all Wales.

At that time the quality of a prince's court was measured by the skill of its bard, and so Prince Elphin was a very proud man. But he went too far when he boasted that Taliesin was a greater bard than any who served the king, Maelgwyn. The king had Elphin cast into a dungeon until the time came when he could prove his boast.

EISTEDDFOD
The National Eisteddfod is an annual festival of Welsh poetry that celebrates the bardic arts of poetry, music, and literature. The word Eisteddfod means "sitting" or "gathering".

Now Taliesin, who was still only a child, went to King Maelgwyn's court, and stood at the door while all the king's bards and courtiers went in. As each one passed him, he cheekily stuck out his lips and played on them with his fingers, "Blerwm, blerwm!"

Then Taliesin entered the court, and when the king asked him who he was, he declared:

> "Primary chief bard am I to Elphin,
> And my original country is the region of the summer stars.
> Once men called me Merlin,
> Soon every king will call me Taliesin.

> "I have been in heaven, I have been in hell,
> I was with Noah when he made the ark.
> I know the names of every star;
> I am a wonder whose origin is not known.

> "I have been in every shape,
> I have been dead, I have been alive.
> I shall be on earth until the day of doom;
> It is not known if I am flesh or fish.

> "I was carried for nine months,
> In the womb of the hag Ceridwen.
> Then I was known as little Gwion,
> But at last I am Taliesin."

Taliesin astonishes the court with his tales

While Elphin languishes in the castle dungeon, King Maelgwyn decides on a contest between his own poet, grey-bearded Heinin, and Taliesin

❖

KING ARTHUR'S BARD
The real Taliesin lived in the 6th century AD. Legend tells that he became court poet to King Arthur.

Maelgwyn summoned his bards to listen. Then he ordered that Elphin, who had been bound with a silver chain, be brought up from the dungeon. While Elphin looked on, Maelgwyn told Heinin, his oldest and wisest bard, to challenge Taliesin to a contest of poetic skill. When Heinin tried to speak, all he could do was flap his fingers across his lips and make a "Blerwm, Blerwm!" sound, like a baby. The same was true for all of the king's bards. Taliesin replied with verses that revealed the world's mysteries and told of things to come.

There was no doubt in King Maelgwyn's mind that Taliesin was indeed the greatest poet in all Wales. He immediately ordered the silver chain to be struck off Elphin, and set the prince free.

GOING TO THE PALACE

One of the most powerful of all the many gods of Voodoo is Ghede, the Lord of Death, who is also known as Baron Samedi. He is the wisest of all the gods, for in his head he holds the knowledge of everyone that has ever lived. If he wishes, he can even bring the dead back to life.

When Ghede steps out of the dark into the light, he needs to wear dark glasses to protect his eyes. But he often takes out the right lens. As he explains, "With my left eye I watch over the whole world, but as for the right, I keep that eye on my food, to make sure that no thief steals it." For Ghede has an enormous appetite. He is a glutton for food, which he shovels into his mouth and swills down with his own special drink, a raw rum steeped in twenty-one hot spices. No one else can bear to swallow it, but Ghede doesn't mind. He will not blink even if the fiery liquid sprays into his eyes.

Sometimes Ghede comes as a ragtag beggarman, but more often he wears formal clothes: a top hat, a long black tailcoat, and a cane. Once, when President Borno ruled Haiti, a whole group of people dressed as Ghede – every one of them a Voodoo priest "ridden" by the spirit of the god himself – marched on the president's palace. They danced and sauntered down the street, singing, with a great crowd following them. They went right past the guards, who were powerless to stop them, through the gates, up the drive, and rapped on the palace door with their canes.

They demanded money, and the president gave plenty to them. For no matter how much power a man may have over other men when he is alive, even the president has no power over death, and in the end must pay his tribute.

Often Ghede sings a song to himself, recalling the day he and his followers danced their way to the palace and made the president pay them to go away:

"Papa Ghede is a handsome fellow,
In his coat and hat of black.
Papa Ghede is going to the palace!
He'll eat and drink when he gets back."

VOODOO DANCERS
In Voodoo ritual, the gods may possess worshippers – "ride" them in ecstatic dance. Voodoo has its roots in West Africa, from where many Haitians were once brought as slaves.

Papa Ghede and his followers set off for the president's palace

THOR IN THE LAND OF GIANTS

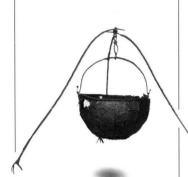

Flame-haired Thor, with his magic hammer, belt, and gloves, drives a chariot pulled by two goats

Thor's hammer, Miollnir

THOR IS THE MIGHTIEST of the Norse gods. Odin is his father; his mother is the Earth. He drives a chariot pulled by two goats, and he has three great treasures: a belt that, when he wears it, doubles his strength; the terrible hammer Miollnir, with which he smites his enemies; and a pair of iron gloves, which he must wear to wield the hammer. Red-bearded god of the sky, Thor is the guardian of Asgard, home of the gods, and of the homes and farmsteads of his worshippers. But even Thor's great strength does not always prevail, as we learn from the story of his visit to the land of the giants, in the company of the trickster, Loki.

"I am tired of lazing around in Asgard," said Thor. "There is nothing here for me to test my strength against."

"There is certainly no point in testing it against my wits," said Loki, "for I would certainly win!"

"Brawn is better than brains," said Thor, "but it needs exercise. How do you think I'd fare in giant-land?"

"There's only one way to find out," said Loki.

So Thor and Loki set off together to look for adventure in the land of the giants. On the first evening of their journey, they stopped at a peasant's hut. The peasant had no food to offer his immortal guests, but Thor slaughtered the two goats who pulled his chariot, and put them in the pot. When the two gods sat down to eat, they invited the peasant and his family to join them.

When all had eaten their fill, Thor placed the goatskins on the floor by the fire and said, "Throw the bones on to the skins." He did not notice Thialfi, the peasant's son, split open a leg bone with his knife, to get at the sweet marrow.

Thor rose with the dawn, and, taking his hammer in his hand, raised it above the goatskins and blessed them, like newborn babies. The goats got up, but one of them was lame in one of its hind legs. Thor's fury knew no bounds. He gripped his hammer so tightly that his knuckles went white. "Someone will pay for this!" he shouted.

COOKING CAULDRON
The Vikings stewed meat in huge cooking pots, or cauldrons. This iron cauldron is from the Oseberg burial ship, in Norway. It hangs on a tripod, which would have been placed over the open fire to cook.

◄ *The Apples of Youth, page 72*

"My apologies, great Thor," mumbled the peasant. "My son acted in ignorance. Take all we have, but spare our lives, I beg you."

When he saw the man cowering in fear, Thor's anger cooled. He accepted, in compensation for the injury to his goat, the peasant's son, Thialfi, and daughter, Roskva, as his servants, and when he and Loki left they took Thialfi and Roskva with them. But they left the goats behind, while the injured goat's leg healed.

They journeyed east until they came to the sea, and crossed it to the land of the giants. When they got there, they found themselves in a deep forest. They walked until dark and at night took refuge in a huge cave with several long passages and one side-chamber. Thor kept guard, his mighty hammer at the ready.

At midnight there was a terrible earthquake, and all night there were rumblings and groanings. They were glad to see the dawn.

In the morning, when they stepped out of the cave, they found a giant, snoring away. The earthquake had been caused by the giant lying down. Thor put on his belt of strength and his iron gloves, and picked up his hammer, but at that moment the giant awoke.

"My name is Skrymir," said the giant, "and I can see that you must be Thor from Asgard. What have you been up to inside my glove?" And Thor saw that the cave in which they had sheltered was indeed Skrymir's glove, and the side-chamber was the thumb.

"We seem to be going in the same direction," said the giant, "and I'm fond of company, so why don't you come with me? If I carry your food in my knapsack, you can keep up with my long strides."

THOR
This small bronze statue of Thor holding his beard (which has turned into his hammer) was found in Iceland. It was made by Vikings in about AD 1000. Thor was the Norse god of thunder. Thursday (Thor's day) is named after him.

Thor and his companions find a safe place to sleep in the forest – little realizing it's a giant's glove

THOR'S HAMMER
Miollnir, Thor's magic hammer, was his main weapon. Charms made in the shape of it brought good luck. This silver one was found in Denmark.

That night, Skrymir came to a halt by a large oak tree. He tossed his knapsack to Thor and stretched out beneath the tree.

Thor busied himself with the knapsack, but whatever he did, he could not get a single knot undone. Hunger and fatigue made him furious, and he took his hammer Miollnir and struck the sleeping giant a fearful blow, right in the centre of his forehead.

Skrymir woke. "What was that?" he asked. "Did a leaf fall on me?" And then he turned over and went back to sleep. So Thor and Loki and Thialfi and Roskva had to go without their supper, and they couldn't sleep either, what with Skrymir snoring so loudly beside them.

At midnight, Thor took up his hammer again and struck another blow. This time he felt the head of the hammer sink

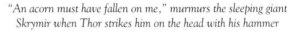

"An acorn must have fallen on me," murmurs the sleeping giant
Skrymir when Thor strikes him on the head with his hammer

into the giant's flesh. But Skrymir only murmured, "An acorn must have fallen on me," before going back to sleep.

Towards dawn, Thor decided that a third blow would surely settle this giant once and for all, so he swung with all his might and buried Miollnir up to the handle in Skrymir's head. But the giant just sat up, saying, "A bird must have dropped a twig on me from a tree. Ah well, it's time to get up, anyway. It's not far now to the giants' citadel at Utgard. There you'll meet some real giants, not little shrimps like me. But watch out: act respectful, or, better still, turn back now!"

Skrymir pointed them on the road to Utgard, and then went on his way, swinging the knapsack behind him. Thor and his companions

❖

SKRYMIR
The nickname given to the giant Skrymir was "Vasty", because he was so enormous. When Thor tried to hammer in Skrymir's skull, the giant merely thought that first a leaf, then an acorn, and finally a twig, had fallen on his head.

were not sorry to see him go, but they did not heed his warning. "We have come too far to turn back now," said Thor.

They soon arrived at Utgard, but found the gates locked. Thor tried with all his strength, but he couldn't open them. By wriggling and squeezing they could just get through the bars and into the courtyard.

They entered a great hall, full of giants who looked at them with sneers of contempt on their faces. The chief of them all, Utgard-Loki, bared his great teeth in a savage grin. "This puny fellow surely cannot be the famous Thor? But perhaps he's stronger than he looks. Whoever you are," he continued, "if you want to stay here, you must entertain us with some feat of strength or skill."

Loki, who was bringing up the rear, piped up, "I'm so hungry I'm sure I could out-eat any giant."

A giant named Logi was chosen to compete with Loki, and a huge dish was fetched and placed on the floor between them. It was piled high with meat. Loki started at one end, and Logi at the other.

Now Loki was famed among gods and men for his ferocious appetite, and he ate all the more hungrily now because he had had no supper

VIKING TRADER
Most Vikings were Christian by the early 11th century; however the Norse gods were not forgotten. This trader wears a Christian cross and a Norse hammer.

Three giants

Logi

Loki

the night before, and no breakfast that day. He gobbled the meat down.

Loki and Logi met exactly in the centre of the dish: a dead heat. Except that where Loki had eaten only the meat, the giant had also consumed the bones and the dish, too. So Loki lost the contest.

Logi and Loki start devouring the meat in the eating contest

The giant Hugi runs so fast that he comes back to meet Thialfi halfway

Next it was Thialfi's turn. Thialfi said he would run a race against anyone, for he was a wiry whippet of a man, and a very fast runner. So a track was cleared, and Thialfi was set to run against a giant named Hugi. Thialfi was so fast at the start that you could barely see him move, but Hugi was faster: so much faster that he turned around at the end of the course and ran back to meet Thialfi half way. So Thialfi, too, lost the contest.

Now it was Thor's turn. "What about a drinking match?" suggested Thor, for he was as thirsty as Loki had been hungry.

The giants brought out a great drinking horn and set it before him. "A good drinker can sink this in one draught," said Utgard-Loki, "though most take two. No one is so feeble as to need three."

No matter how much Thor drinks, he cannot empty the drinking horn

DRINKING HORN
At their feasts, the Vikings drank mead, an alcoholic drink made of fermented honey and water. They drank from horns, which were made from polished ox-horn or metal. The drinking horn could not be put down when full without overturning, so the drinker had to down the liquid in one gulp. The drinking horn above is a copy of one found in Jutland, Denmark, and later destroyed. The raised figures on the horn would have been added by craftsmen.

Thor did not think the horn looked as big as all that, so he set to, glugging the drink down in great gulps. But when he stopped, out of breath, the level in the horn was hardly lower than before. He tried again, but the level only fell a tiny bit. Thor tried a third time. He drank till he thought he would burst, but when he stopped, spluttering and out of breath, the horn was still not empty.

There was scorn in Utgard-Loki's voice. "Who would have thought that the great Thor was so feeble? It scarcely seems worth your while trying any other feat."

Thor tries with all his strength to lift the grey cat off the ground

"I'll try anything," said Thor.

"There is a simple game some of our youngsters play," said Utgard-Loki. "There's nothing to it, really. You just lift that grey cat off the ground. I wouldn't suggest it to a man of your reputation, except you really don't seem as strong as people say."

Thor went to the cat and put his arms around its belly and pulled. He pulled and pulled with all his strength, and the cat arched its back higher and higher until, as Thor's strength finally gave way, he did lift one of its paws from the ground. But that was all he could do.

"Never mind," said Utgard-Loki, in his silkiest voice. "After all, it is rather a big cat."

Thor was, by this time, in a raging fury. "If you think I am such a weakling, why doesn't one of you come and fight," he cried.

"You can't expect a self-respecting giant to fight someone who can't even lift up a cat," said Utgard-Loki. "But if you like, you can wrestle with my old nurse, Elli."

A withered old crone came into the hall and adopted a wrestler's stance. Thor seized her and tried to throw her to the floor, but however much he heaved and strained, he could not move her. Then, with unexpected strength, the old woman forced him on to one knee.

Utgard-Loki shouted, "Stop the fight! There's no point in continuing. Still, Thor and his companions have tried their best."

❖

VIKING CONTESTS
The Vikings were fiercely competitive people who loved to play games and take part in contests. Norse myths such as this one reflect their fighting natures.

The old crone forces Thor on to one knee

The land around the castle of Utgard shows the marks of Thor's hammer.

The next morning, Utgard-Loki accompanied Thor and his companions on the road back towards Asgard.

"I have been made fun of," said Thor. "How can I hold my head up among the gods?"

"I will tell you how," said Utgard-Loki. "We giants had heard of your strength and prowess and, in truth, we were not eager to try ourselves against you. Therefore I myself met you in the forest, under the name of Skrymir, which means "Big Lad". If you look near my castle, you will see three great valleys. Those are the marks of your hammer blows. You thought you were hitting me, but you were deceived. So, too, in the contests. Loki's opponent was Flame, who devours everything in his path. Thialfi ran against Thought, which is the quickest thing of all. And as for you, Thor, when you were drinking from the horn, you did not realize that the other end was in the sea. No one could drink the ocean dry, but you have lowered it. And from now on, twice each day the sea will empty and then refill, in memory of your heroic draughts.

"As for the cat, to raise one of its paws was an even greater feat, for the cat was the Midgard serpent, which encircles the whole earth.

"But the wrestling match showed your true strength. For the crone Elli was Old Age, and there never has been anyone, and never will be, that old age cannot beat."

Thor was furious to hear how he had been tricked, and reached for his hammer to teach Utgard-Loki a lesson: but the giant was nowhere to be seen. Thor stormed back towards the castle, intending to smash it to the ground, but he found only green fields and grey sky.

So Thor and his companions returned to Asgard. "The cunning will always defeat the strong," said Loki.

"Tell that to my hammer," growled Thor.

DEEP CHASM
Cracks and crevasses are a feature of Iceland's landscape. However, they were probably not caused by blows from Thor's mighty hammer, but by volcanic activity deep under the ground.

The Death of Balder, page 162 ➤

CUCHULAIN

CONCHUBAR, KING OF ULSTER, had one hundred and fifty boys in his service. This is how he passed every day: one third of the day watching the boys at play; one third playing a board game called fidchell; and one third drinking until he fell asleep.

Idle King Conchubar spends his days playing fidchell, watching his boys fighting – and drinking

King Conchubar

Young Cuchulain begs his mother to be allowed to go and fight with the older boys

Conchubar's nephew, Cuchulain, begged his mother to be allowed to join the boys. "You are too young," she answered, for he was only six. "Wait awhile." But Cuchulain would not wait. He set out with his stick and ball and his toy javelin and shield. He could throw the javelin ahead and run forward to catch it before it fell to the ground.

When he arrived at the playing fields, the boys laughed at him and told him to go away. They threw their javelins at him, but he warded them off with his toy shield.

The boys laugh and throw spears at him, but Cuchulain wards them off with his toy shield

❖

THE ULSTER CYCLE
Cuchulain is the hero of the Ulster Cycle of myths, which dates from the 7th century AD.

When they attacked Cuchulain, for the first time his battle fury came upon him. His hair seemed on fire. One eye closed, and shrank back into his head; the other eye glared, and stood out on a stalk. His snarl split his face from jaw to ear. His mouth stretched open so you could see right down his throat. Behind his head was a glare of red. He chased the boys all the way to where Conchubar was playing fidchell. And Conchubar took Cuchulain into his service, for the boy was the son of the king's sister. Some said his father was Lugh, the Master of Many Arts, a chieftain of the godlike Tuatha de Danaan, Ireland's first rulers.

Cuchulain achieved many great feats and became known as the Hound of Ulster. He grew into a handsome young man – except in his battle fury. His hair was brown at the base, blood-red in the middle, and golden yellow at the ends. King Conchubar, seeing what a fine young man his nephew had become, sent nine men out into the provinces of Ireland to find a suitable bride for him. But when they returned, none of them had found a girl fine enough for Cuchulain.

So Cuchulain himself set out, dressed in his best clothes – a white linen shirt, a crimson tunic, and a brooch of fine gold – to court Emer, the daughter of Forgall Manach the Wily. Emer was the loveliest girl in the whole of Ireland. She flirted with the young warrior and matched him wit for wit. And they pledged themselves to each other.

Now Forgall Manach was not pleased that his daughter should throw herself away on a mere warrior, especially one who, because of his horrifying battle fury, was known as the Warped One. And Forgall

Enraged by the boys' teasing, Cuchulain's battle fury comes upon him for the first time in his life, transforming the handsome young lad into a fearsome sight

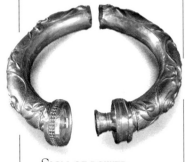

SIGN OF POWER
This tubular collar, called a torque, was worn around the neck by wealthy men and women. Gold torques, such as the one above, belonged only to the most powerful. As well as being a sign of rank, a warrior's torque brought him good luck in battle.

Cuchulain and Emer pledge their love – against the wishes of her father, Forgall the Wily

was not called the Wily for nothing. He went to King Conchubar and praised Cuchulain mightily for his great prowess in the arts of war. "But," he said, " he will never reach his full power unless he studies under Scathach, the Scottish warrior-woman." Forgall knew that no man had ever survived as Scathach's pupil, for she was the greatest warrior there had ever been.

As soon as Cuchulain heard this suggestion, he went in search of Scathach. She lived on an island, and the only way on to it was over a high bridge that, when a man stood on it, bucked like a frightened horse. Cuchulain made his hero's salmon-leap on to the middle of the bridge, and sprang off it again before he could be flung into the water.

Scathach accepted him as her pupil and taught him all the arts of war. She taught him the feats of the sword edge and the sloped shield, the cat's twist and the hero's scream, the blow that stuns and the

WARRIOR OF STONE
This stone bust of an Irish warrior, perhaps a chieftain or a god, comes from Tandaragee, County Armagh, Northern Ireland. It stands 60 cm (2 ft) high and dates from the 1st century AD. The bumps on the soldier's helmet could be the remains of a pair of horns.

Cuchulain springs across the magic bridge using his hero's salmon-leap and becomes the pupil of Scathach, the formidable warrior-woman

stroke that severs. Alone of all her pupils, she taught him the *gae bolga*, the lightning spear-thrust no enemy could withstand.

Then Cuchulain left Scathach and rode in his chariot to Forgall's fortress. Forgall barred the gate against him, but Cuchulain leapt the walls. Forgall fell to his death trying to escape the hero's fury, and Cuchulain took the lovely Emer for his wife.

RIDING HIGH
Irish warriors sallied forth into battle in beautifully decorated, horse-drawn chariots. These bronze mounts, inlaid with red enamel, would have adorned a horse's harness.

Now the men of Ireland in those days were great ones for fighting, and almost any excuse would do. And so it was that the armies of Ireland went to war when King Ailill and Queen Maeve of Connaught tried to steal away a fine prize, the great bull of Ulster.

Cuchulain

Alone, Cuchulain takes on the armies of Ireland

King Ailill and Queen Maeve steal the great bull of Ulster

Cuchulain's mother sees her son's wine turn to blood and realizes he is doomed

STANDING STONES
The Leganny dolmen (stone table) of County Down in Northern Ireland, may have been an ancient tomb. The dying Cuchulain must have strapped himself to similar stones.

At that time the men of Ulster were under a spell – struck down by weakness and pain so severe that they could not fight. Only Cuchulain was unaffected. Alone, he stood at a ford and held off the armies of Connaught and the other Irish provinces. First he challenged all the best warriors and killed them all. Then he took to his chariot and attacked the armies. He killed so many men that the battle that day is one of the three uncountable slaughters of Ireland.

The enmity between the men of Ulster and the other provinces of Ireland was not ended by Cuchulain's great deeds – it grew worse. And the day came when Cuchulain readied himself to fight them once again. He went to his mother to bid her goodbye, and she gave him a cup of wine in farewell. But when he came to drink it, there was only blood in the cup. Three times she rinsed the cup and filled it with wine; three times the wine turned into blood. "My luck has turned against me," said Cuchulain. "I will not come back alive."

Cuchulain's mother begged him to stay with her that day until his luck returned but he said, "I have never turned from a battle and I never will. A great name is better than a long life."

On his way to the battle, Cuchulain saw a young girl with white skin and red hair – one of the fairy folk, the Sidhe, – weeping at a ford. She was washing and washing a bundle of red-stained clothes. Cathbad the druid, who was with him, told him, "Those are your clothes she is washing. She is crying because she knows you are going to your death."

But Cuchulain did not turn back. He came upon the armies of Ireland in his chariot and slew them by the hundred. They fell like the leaves from the trees in autumn, and stained the plain red with their blood. But at last Lugaid, son of Curoi, drove a spear through Cuchulain's belly, and Cuchulain knew that he had received his death-wound.

He asked leave to go down to the lake and take a mouthful of water, and Lugaid granted his wish. Cuchulain went down to the water and drank and washed himself. Then he turned back to face his death.

In the middle of the battle plain there was a great standing stone, and Cuchulain tied himself to that stone with his breast-belt, so that he would die on his feet. He continued to fight until a crow landed on his shoulder, the bird of the war goddess Morrigan, or maybe even the goddess herself, and then Lugaid dealt the death-stroke.

And that was the passing of the mighty Cuchulain, the Hound of Ulster.

Riding to the battle with Cathbad the druid, Cuchulain glimpses a weeping fairy girl washing bloodstained clothes

Cathbad

Lugaid

Resolved to die on his feet like a hero, Cuchulain lashes himself to a standing stone. But as a crow flaps around his helpless body, his enemy, Lugaid, prepares to strike

THE LABOURS OF HERACLES

**HERA**
Zeus's wife, Hera, was the most powerful Greek goddess, and the patron of wedded love. Her jealous nature led her to take revenge on many of Zeus's lovers.

GREAT ZEUS, KING OF the gods, had many love affairs with mortal women, much to the distress of his wife, the goddess Hera. The children born of these love affairs were half gods themselves and, of them all, none was greater than Heracles, for he was conceived to be the protector of both men and gods.

Zeus lay with Alcmene, Heracles' mother, in the guise of her husband, Amphitryon, who was away at the wars. Zeus commanded time itself to slow down, so that one night was the length of three. When Amphitryon returned the following day, Alcmene was too tired to welcome him home; she was already carrying Zeus's child.

Nine months later, Zeus boasted in Olympus of the hero, his son, who was about to be born. "His name will be Heracles, and he will rule the noble House of Perseus."

Hera was furious, especially as the name Heracles means, "Glory of Hera". She went to Zeus and asked him, "Do you swear that the child to be born to the House of Perseus today will be king of Mycenae?"

"I swear," said Zeus.

Hera at once went to Mycenae, and there she hastened the birth of Eurystheus, Heracles's cousin. Then she went and sat outside the door of Alcmene's bedchamber and bewitched her so that she could not give birth until the next day. Zeus could not go back on his word, so Eurystheus, instead of Heracles, became king. However, Hera agreed that if Heracles could perform twelve Labours to be set by Eurystheus, he could become a god. Alcmene was so frightened at finding herself in the middle of a quarrel between Zeus and Hera that she abandoned her baby outside Thebes, Mycenae's main city.

Zeus, seeing what had happened, asked the goddess Athena to take Hera past the spot.

"Look at this strong child," Athena exclaimed. "His mother must be mad to leave him. You're nursing, Hera. Give him a drink."

And so, by letting the baby drink from her breast, Hera was tricked into saving Heracles's life. Athena later returned the baby to Alcmene. "Guard him well," she said.

Fearing Hera's anger, Alcmene abandons the baby Heracles outside the city walls

A year later, Hera tried again to foil the plans of Zeus. She sent two fearful serpents, with rippling blue scales and flame-filled eyes, to sink their poisoned fangs into the infant as he slept.

In the morning, Alcmene found Heracles sitting up, gurgling with pleasure, and dangling the dead serpents over the sides of his bed. He had strangled them with his bare hands.

This was just one of the amazing feats performed by Heracles in childhood. He grew straight and tall, with fiery eyes and strength beyond his years. He liked to roam under the stars, and learned to think as well as to fight. He was an expert with both bow and javelin, but his favoured weapon was a club cut from a wild olive tree.

Young Heracles strangles the deadly serpents with his bare hands

OLIVE TREE, CORFU Heracles (known to the Romans as Hercules) cut his favourite wooden club from the olive tree. This evergreen, highly prized in ancient times, grows well in Mediterranean countries.

At last the time came for Heracles to undertake the twelve Labours that would make him a god. The first task set by Eurystheus was intended to be the last, for he asked his cousin to kill the Nemean lion, a fearsome beast whose thick hide was proof against any weapon.

When Heracles arrived in Nemea, he could not find anyone to tell him where the lion was, for it had devoured everyone in its path. So he hunted it across the country and tracked it to its lair. There he waited, until the lion returned from hunting, its mane flecked with the blood of its victims.

Heracles shot at the lion with his bow, but his arrows just bounced off. He swung at it with his sword, but the weapon rebounded in his hands. So he followed the creature into its cave and there he seized it in his arms, and throttled it to death.

When Heracles returned to Thebes, wearing the lion's pelt as armour, King Eurystheus nearly fainted away. "Next time," he said, "just send me word that you have achieved your task. There is no need to come in person."

For Eurystheus was terrified that what his cousin could do to the Nemean lion, he might also do to a Theban king.

Heracles wrestles with the Nemean lion, slowly throttling it to death

Several of the Labours of Heracles were similar in nature – he was
sent to fight a monster and succeeded, by strength and guile, in
killing or capturing it. His second task was to kill the many-headed
Hydra, a creature so terrible that to smell its breath was fatal. Each
time he cut off one of its heads, it grew more. But at last he killed it.

In this way, Heracles was sent against the Cerynean hind, the
Erymanthian boar, the Stymphalian birds, the Cretan bull, the mares
of Diomedes, and the cattle of Geryon. He was also sent to steal the
golden girdle of the Amazon queen Hippolyta, which Eurystheus
wanted to give to his daughter, Admete.

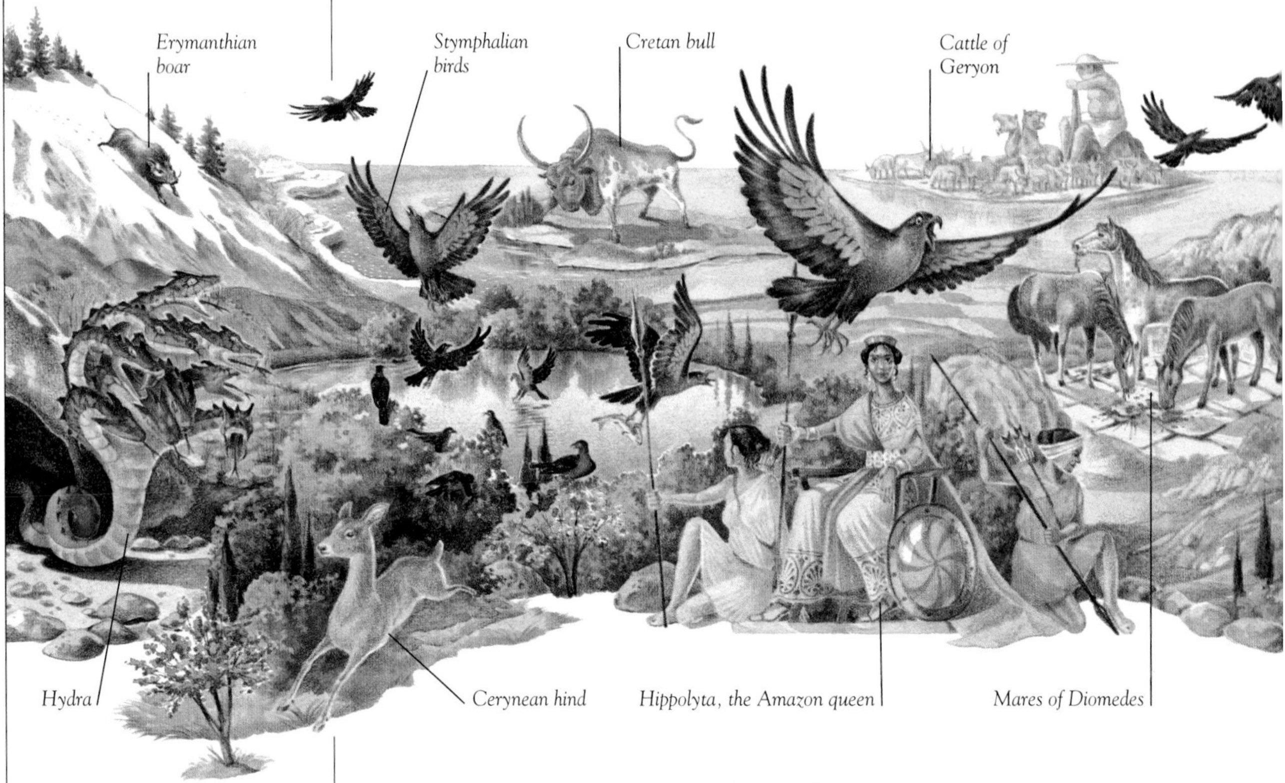

Erymanthian
boar

Stymphalian
birds

Cretan bull

Cattle of
Geryon

Hydra

Cerynean hind

Hippolyta, the Amazon queen

Mares of Diomedes

All these tasks Heracles achieved. But the three that remained were
of a different nature.

"It is clear that he can hunt and fight," said Eurystheus. "But let's
see how he likes hard work."

Heracles was sent to clean the stables of King Augeus, and
Eurystheus and his courtiers burst with laughter at the thought, for
the Augean stables had not been cleaned in living history. The dung
of the cattle and horses lay in such great mounds that the buildings
were pretty well covered in manure.

"He won't be able to look down his nose at me after a year or two of dung-carrying," joked Eurystheus, "even if he is the son of a god. He won't want to use his nose at all!"

But Heracles was not daunted. When he arrived at the stables, he told King Augeus, "I'll have it done by nightfall."

The first thing that Heracles did was to make two breaches in the stable walls. Then he diverted two nearby rivers so that they ran through the stables, and within a day they had swept the stables, and

The Garden of the Hesperides

Heracles wears the pelt of the Nemean lion as armour

Stables of King Augeus

the fields and valleys, clean again. And so Heracles removed the mountains of dung without soiling his hands at all.

The eleventh Labour was more tricky. Heracles was sent to fetch some golden apples from the Garden of the Hesperides, which can be found in the far west where the sun sets, on the slopes of Mount Atlas. The apples grew on a tree that was a wedding present to the goddess Hera from Gaia, mother of the earth. It was tended by three maidens, the Hesperides. In addition, a fierce serpent was coiled round the tree, to protect the precious fruit from thieves.

❖

LEGENDARY LINES
Today, a very hard task may be descibed as "Herculean" after the Labours of Heracles; and writers may mention the Augean Stables when describing a filthy place.

❖

THE GOLDEN APPLES
The Hesperides guarded the golden apples, which were given to Hera by the earth mother Gaia. The apples gave eternal life to those who ate them.

❖
ATLAS'S BURDEN
Atlas was one of the defeated Titans, who was sentenced by the Olympian gods to carry the sky on his shoulders as a punishment. His three daughters, the Hesperides, looked after the golden apples in their garden.

Atlas bears the weight of the heavens on his shoulders

Heracles was baffled as to how to steal this treasure and decided to take counsel from the gods. He was told that only Nereus, the Old Man of the Sea, knew how to find the Garden of the Hesperides. Heracles seized Nereus while he slept and held grimly on to him, even though Nereus changed his shape many times trying to escape. Eventually, Nereus told him everything he needed to know.

Instead of going straight to the Garden, Heracles approached Atlas, whose everlasting task it was to hold up the heavens on his shoulders. "You must be tired of bearing such a heavy weight," Heracles said. "If you'll do something for me, I'll take a turn for a while."

"What must I do?" asked Atlas eagerly.

"Only fetch for me the golden apples that your three daughters tend. Surely they will give them to you."

"My daughters may give me the apples, but the serpent that guards the tree will certainly kill me."

"I will shoot the serpent with my bow, from outside the garden."

"In that case, I shall do as you ask."

So Heracles killed the serpent, and took up the burden of Atlas. When Atlas returned with the apples, he was whistling a happy tune. "It is good to walk freely in the world again," he said. "I'll take these apples to Eurystheus myself. You're a big strong lad, quite capable of holding up the heavens in my stead."

Heracles had been warned by Nereus that this would happen. He said, "After all you've done for me, I'd be delighted. But I can already feel the heavens rubbing a sore spot on my head. If you'll just take them back for a moment, I'll make myself a pad out of grass."

Atlas set down the apples and took the heavens back from Heracles. But instead of making a pad, Heracles just picked up the apples and walked away.

"Thank you!" he called.

In the garden of the Hesperides, a serpent guards the golden apples

The twelfth Labour of Heracles was the most difficult of all. He had to descend to Hades, the Underworld, and bring back the watchdog of hell, Cerberus, who had three heads. It was Cerberus's job to keep the dead in Hades, and the living out.

When Heracles descended to the Underworld, he saw many friends and legendary heroes of long ago, who seemed to welcome, or to threaten him. But he knew they were mere shades, and ignored them in his quest for the dog.

He was greeted by Hades himself, and his wife, Persephone. Hades laughed and said, "The dog is yours, if you can take him." And Heracles, gathering all his courage, threw his powerful arms around the dog, throttling it as he had done the Nemean lion at the start of his adventures, and dragged it up into the world of day.

Cerberus whined and snarled all the way into the light, and where the flecks of slaver that flew from its mouth fell to the ground, poisonous aconites grew.

When Heracles arrived at Tiryns with the dog, his cousin Eurystheus was so terrified he begged him to take it back where it had come from. And that was the end of Heracles's Labours.

In the end, death came to the mortal part of Heracles when he put on a shirt accidentally soaked in poison by his wife. However, his immortal part, which lives for ever, could not be conquered. While his mortal shade wanders in Hades, his immortal self guards the door of Heaven.

It is said that when Heracles ascended to join the gods, Atlas staggered under the extra weight.

Heracles descends into the Underworld to find the three-headed dog, Cerberus

The Winged Horse, page 148 ➤

GODS AND ANIMALS

Humans have always shared the world with animals and, as prehistoric cave paintings attest, animals have always exerted an endless fascination over people's minds. We have hunted animals, worked with them, and even worshipped them. The ancient Egyptians so revered cats, that when one died it was mourned, mummified, and entombed with mummified mice to eat in the hereafter.

The myths of the world reflect every facet of our relationship with real animals, as well as telling tales of fabulous beasts, such as Pegasus, the winged horse, and the Phoenix, the immortal bird of harmony.

Quetzalcoatl, the serpent god, recoils in horror when he sees he has been given a human face in The Plumed Serpent, *a story that places the innocence of animals above the lusts of humans*

ROMULUS AND REMUS

N UMITOR, KING OF ALBA, had been ousted by his brutal brother, Amulius. Amulius made sure Numitor would have no heirs by forcing Numitor's only child, his daughter, Rhea Silvia, to spend her days as a vestal virgin, serving in the temple of Vesta, goddess of the hearth. Nevertheless Rhea subsequently gave birth to twin boys, Romulus and Remus. Their father was not a man, but Mars, god of war. When Amulius found out what had happened, he slew Rhea Silvia and had the two boys thrown into the River Tiber.

The river bore the twins safely ashore, where they were found by a she-wolf who suckled them with her milk.

THE ETERNAL CITY
According to legend, Romulus and Remus founded Rome, "The Eternal City", in 753 BC. They built the city on seven hills near the River Tiber in what is now Italy.

Faustulus the shepherd comes upon the twins, Romulus and Remus, being suckled by a she-wolf

ROMAN GAMES
Athleticism, skill, and bravery were tested in organized games, which were hugely popular with the Romans. This mosaic from the 3rd century AD shows two women athletes.

The wolf looked after them until they were found by Faustulus, one of the old king's shepherds, who adopted them as his own.

When the boys were grown, Faustulus told them who their father was and described their mother's fate. Romulus and Remus avenged her by killing Amulius, and they restored Numitor to the throne.

They then decided to build a city on the River Tiber. Realizing that only one of them could be its ruler, they sought guidance from the gods. Each climbed a high mountain, to see what he could see. Remus saw a flight of six vultures, but Romulus saw twelve. Therefore Romulus, judging that the gods had favoured him, began to lay the foundations of the city of Rome. He ploughed a furrow to mark where the walls would be. But Remus mocked him, leaping over the thin furrow and saying that Rome's enemies would be able to get over its walls just as easily. Romulus was so furious he struck his brother dead.

The city was built. It had a ruler, but no citizens. So Romulus declared Rome's sacred grove to be sanctuary, and it soon filled with

Remus mocks the thin furrow that Romulus is digging

outlaws and fugitives, whom Romulus welcomed as his subjects.

But there were still no women. So Romulus organized some games and invited his neighbours, the Sabines. While the Sabine men were enjoying themselves, he and his men carried off many of the Sabine women to Rome. Bloody war followed, but eventually the women themselves stopped the fighting, begging their new husbands and their fathers not to slaughter themselves needlessly.

Romulus, the founder of Rome, was not to be its earthly ruler for long. For his father, Mars, begged almighty Jupiter to make Romulus a god. When Jupiter agreed, Mars descended in his chariot and swept Romulus away. The body of the living man melted into thin air, and he became a god. From heaven, Romulus oversaw the rise, and fall, of the great nation he had founded.

Having distracted the Sabine menfolk, Romulus and his men seize the Sabine women and carry them off to Rome

THE PLUMED SERPENT

QUETZALCOATL'S MASK
This 15th-century turquoise mosaic mask represents Quetzalcoatl, the Aztec god of creation, learning, and the wind. The Aztecs believed that they lived beneath the sun of Quetzalcoatl, the plumed serpent god. The sun moved only when carried by his breath. When warriors died, their souls became rare feathered birds after four years, and flew to meet this sun.

❖

TEZCATLIPOCA
According to Aztec myth, Tezcatlipoca was the god of warriors, the night sky, and the thunderbolt. His name, "smoking mirror", comes from his magic mirror, in which he could see everything, as well as read people's thoughts.

Q UETZALCOATL, THE SERPENT GOD, was the king of the City of the Gods. He was totally pure, innocent, and good. No task was too humble for him. He even swept the paths for the rain gods, so that they might come and rain.

Quetzalcoatl's cunning brother, Tezcatlipoca, was infuriated by his perfect goodness. With some friends, Tezcatlipoca decided to play a dirty trick on Quetzalcoatl and turn him into a pleasure-seeking rascal. "We will give him a human face and body," he grinned.

They showed Quetzalcoatl his new features in a smoking mirror. As soon as Quetzalcoatl looked into the mirror and saw his face, he felt himself possessed by all the worldly desires that afflict mankind.

Tezcatlipoca shows Quetzalcoatl his new, human face and body in a smoking mirror

Tezcatlipoca pours wine into a bowl to give to Quetzalcoatl

Quetzalcoatl drinks the wine and makes love to his sister, Quetzalpetatl

Xolotl, the coyote, makes Quetzalcoatl a coat of green, red, and white feathers

He cried out in horror. "I am no longer fit to be king. I cannot appear like this before my people." He called the coyote Xolotl to him. Xolotl, who was as close to Quetzalcoatl as his own shadow, made him a coat of green, red, and white feathers from the Quetzal bird. He also made him a turquoise mask, and a wig and beard of blue and red feathers. He reddened the king's lips, painted his forehead with yellow dye, and drew on his teeth to make them look like serpent's teeth. And so Quetzalcoatl was disguised as a plumed serpent.

However, Tezcatlipoca had thought of a new trick to play on his brother. He gave Quetzalcoatl wine, telling him it was a potion to cure his malady. Quetzalcoatl, who had never drunk alcohol before, soon became drunk. While he was in a stupor, Tezcatlipoca persuaded him to make love to his own sister, the beautiful Quetzalpetatl.

When Quetzalcoatl awoke, he was bitterly ashamed of what he had done. "This is an evil day," he said, and he resolved to die.

COYOTE
This Toltec ornament, which is covered with mother-of-pearl mosaic, represents a warrior from the Toltec city of Tula. It shows a man's head held in the jaws of a coyote. Xolotl, the coyote, was the Aztec god of the evening star. The name Xolotl means "twin", and so the god is often referred to as Quetzalcoatl's double, or twin brother.

Quetzalcoatl ordered his servants to make a stone box, and he lay in it for four days. Then he arose and told the servants to fill the box with all his rarest treasures and seal it up.

Quetzalcoatl went to the sea and there he put on his coat of quetzal feathers and his turquoise mask. And then he set fire to himself until there was nothing left but ashes on the shore. From these ashes, rare birds rose into the sky.

When Quetzalcoatl died, the dawn did not rise for four days, because Quetzalcoatl had descended to the land of the dead with his double, Xolotl, to see his father, Mictlantecuhtli. He told his father, the Lord of the Dead, "I have come to take the precious bones that you have here to people the Earth."

And the Lord of the Dead replied, "It is well."

QUETZAL BIRD
This colourful bird from Central America is associated with the plumed serpent god, Quetzalcoatl. The Aztec people used the bird's long tail feathers in their ceremonies.

Quetzalcoatl's servants fill the stone box with his treasures

Rare birds rise from the ashes of Quetzalcoatl's funeral pyre

❖

KING QUETZALCOATL
A king named Quetzalcoatl ruled the Toltecs, who were conquered by the Aztecs. He was a man of exceptional gifts, similar to the King Arthur of Celtic myth. The Aztecs believed they were his successors and many legends grew up about him.

Quetzalcoatl and Xolotl took the precious bones, and made their way back to the land of the living. As dawn rose once more, Quetzalcoatl sprinkled his blood over the bones and gave them life. The bones became the first people.

Quetzalcoatl taught humankind many important things. He found maize, which the ants had hidden, and stole a grain of it to give to the people he had created so that they could grow food for themselves. He taught them how to polish jade, how to weave fabrics, and make mosaics. Best of all he taught them how to measure time and understand the stars, and he laid down the course of the year and the seasons.

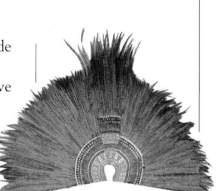

FEATHER HEADDRESS
This headdress, made from Quetzal birds' feathers, belonged to Montezuma, the last Aztec ruler. In 1519 he gave the headdress to the Spanish adventurer Cortes, thinking he was Quetzalcoatl returned. Two years later, the Spanish had conquered his whole empire.

Quetzalcoatl

Quetzalcoatl teaches people how to weave, polish jade, and make mosaics

Quetzalcoatl and Xolotl make each person out of bones from the land of the dead

Xolotl

At last it was time for Quetzalcoatl to leave humans to fend for themselves. When that day dawned, there appeared in the sky the star Quetzalcoatl, which we know as Venus. For this reason Quetzalcoatl is called Lord of the Dawn. Some say Quetzalcoatl sailed to the east on a raft of serpents, and one day he will return.

Quetzalcoatl sails away

THE ELEPHANT GOD

ART MASTER
Shiva is often portrayed
as destructive, but he
also has peaceful forms.
This bronze statuette
shows Shiva as
Vinadhara, "Master of
the Arts".

ALL MEN HAVE THE GOD SHIVA in their soul, just as all women have the goddess Devi, who is sometimes called Parvati. The ebb and flow of the universe, which moves and is still, is the union of Shiva and Parvati.

Now Parvati, as Shiva's wife, wanted to have children. But Shiva, who was free from all passions, did not feel the same way. "I can never die," he said, "so I have no need for a son to make offerings to my soul. It is enough for me that we can enjoy helping men and women to make children. We don't need our own." But Parvati longed for a child, and she fell into a terrible sadness.

Shiva is jealous of the new arrival

The bundle of cloth Parvati cradles in her arms turns into a baby, Ganesha

When Shiva saw how much she wanted a child, he told her, "There is no need to pine. If you want a son to kiss, I will give you one." And he made a bundle out of material from her dress, and gave it to her. "There is a son for you," he said.

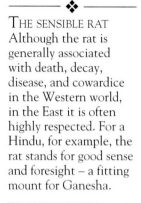

The goddess clutched the bundle of cloth to her breast. Suddenly it quivered with life. She caressed it with lotus flowers. It began to breathe. It was a real baby, calling out for the milk from her breast.

As the baby drank, he smiled up at his mother.

But Shiva was not pleased that his cloth-baby had come to life. Jealous of all the attention the new arrival was getting from his wife, he scowled at the child – and the burning rays of Shiva's middle eye scorched away the baby's head!

THE SENSIBLE RAT

Although the rat is generally associated with death, decay, disease, and cowardice in the Western world, in the East it is often highly respected. For a Hindu, for example, the rat stands for good sense and foresight – a fitting mount for Ganesha.

Given a new head by Shiva, Ganesha thrives as the elephant god of good fortune

GANESHA

Indian schoolchildren often have the god's picture on the covers of their exercise books, to bring them good luck. Ganesha is often pictured carrying a weapon, a warning for those that fail to pay him respect.

Parvati was beside herself with grief, so Shiva guiltily looked around for another head. The nearest creature was a one-tusked elephant. Shiva quickly cut off its head and gave it to the child.

And that is how the little pot-bellied god, Ganesha, who rides around this world on a rat, and is the patron of learning and the giver of good fortune, comes to have the head of an elephant.

Ganesha's mount is a rat, an animal renowned for its good sense

THE CAT GODDESS

BASTET
This figurine of Bastet the cat goddess shows her with kittens at her feet, emphasizing her link with fertility. In one hand she carries a sistrum, a percussion instrument, in the other she has an image of the lion goddess Sekhmet, her dangerous aspect.

THE NILE
The sacred cats of old Egypt got their fish from the Nile. The river's regular floods created a highly fertile valley that enabled a civilization to flourish.

IN ANCIENT EGYPT, all cats were sacred. If a house was on fire, the owners would save the household cat before anything else. It was death to kill a cat.

The cat deity, who each night saved Re, the sun god, from Apep, serpent of chaos, came to be called Bastet. She was a love goddess, full of the sun's warmth.

The centre of her worship was the city of Bubastis, which boasted a fine temple in her honour. Each spring, the citizens would go out of the city and sail back in ships, playing drums and pipes, singing and clapping. The merrymaking would go on all night. Cats going about their business would add their voices in praise of Bastet.

The people of Bubastis celebrate the springtime festival dedicated to the cat goddess Bastet

KING OF THE BIRDS

ONCE UPON A TIME, in the first cycle of the world's history, the four-legged creatures chose the lion as their king, the fishes chose the monster-fish Ananda, and the birds chose the golden mallard duck. This golden mallard was one of the early forms of the Buddha, who was born many times, in many shapes, both human and animal, before he at last achieved release from the wheel of life. Always he showed wisdom, leadership, and humility, and there are many lessons to be learned from the stories of his lives, which are known as the Jataka tales. Even when he was born as an outcast pariah dog, living on scraps he found among the rubbish, the Buddha became leader of all the stray dogs, and earned the king's favour.

Now the king golden mallard had a lovely daughter, who was the apple of his eye. She asked him to allow her to choose her own husband, and he agreed. He summoned all the birds to a plateau of bare rock high in the mountains of the Himalayas so that she could make her choice. Every single bird came.

As the king's daughter inspected the vast flock of birds, her eye was caught by the shimmering, many-hued beauty of the peacock. "This one shall be my husband," she said.

When the peacock heard this, he was overcome with pride and vanity. He danced and he pranced; he spread his wings and fanned out his beautiful tail, displaying himself for all to see.

DUCK TILES
The golden ducks on these tiles from the Man Singh palace in Gwalior, northern India, symbolize the Buddha, founder of the Buddhist religion.

The king mallard declared, "This bird has no modesty in his heart or decency in his bearing. My daughter shall never marry such a vain wretch."

So instead the king gave his daughter to a young mallard, his nephew, and the peacock flew away in shame.

Human vanity often causes people to lose a treasure that is nearly within their grasp.

The king mallard decides that his daughter shall marry his modest nephew

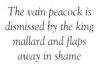

The vain peacock is dismissed by the king mallard and flaps away in shame

THE WINGED HORSE

BIRTH OF PEGASUS
This story tells how the Greek hero Perseus killed the fearsome Medusa, releasing Pegasus, the winged horse (shown in the relief above). It also tells how Pegasus later became the mount of Bellerophon in his quest to kill the terrible Chimaera.

A CRISIUS, KING OF ARGOS, had only one child, a daughter called Danae. He wanted a son, and asked the oracle what the future held. The oracle replied: "You will have no son and your grandson will kill you." The terrified king locked his daughter away in a high tower behind doors of brass. However, the god Zeus came to her in a shower of gold, and, in time, she bore a son, Perseus.

Fearing Zeus's wrath if he killed his daughter and grandson, Acrisius cast Danae and Perseus adrift on the sea in a wooden chest. Danae prayed to Zeus for help and, instead of being swamped by the waves, their chest was washed up on the island of Seriphos.

At length, the island's king, Polydectes, met Danae. He desired to marry her, but she refused him. With Perseus, who was by now fully grown, to protect her, the king knew he would never bend her to his will. He decided to get rid of Perseus. He held a banquet for the island's young men. All the guests brought gifts, except Perseus, who was too poor. Ashamed, he promised the king a present. "Bring me the head of the Gorgon Medusa," Polydectes sniggered. Medusa was a terrible monster, with snakes for hair and a glance that turned people to stone. The task was impossible.

Zeus took pity on Perseus and sent two Immortals, Athena and Hermes, to him. Athena lent Perseus her polished shield, saying: "Look only on Medusa's reflection in the shield and you will not be turned to stone." Hermes lent Perseus a sickle to cut off the Gorgon's head. He also told Perseus how to find the Nymphs of the North Wind, who would lend him winged sandals, a wallet to hold Medusa's head, and fetch for him the Cap of Invisibility from Hades, god of the Underworld.

When Perseus cuts off Medusa's head, Pegasus springs from her body

Wearing sandals and cap, Perseus flew unseen to the far west. He found Medusa and her two sisters asleep among the weatherworn statues of other heroes, all turned to stone by her glare. Looking only at Medusa's reflection in his shield, Perseus swung the sickle, cut off her head and thrust it into the wallet. From her body sprang the marvellous winged horse, Pegasus.

On his way home, Perseus saw a girl chained to a rock. Her name was Andromeda and she was about to be sacrificed to a sea monster, to prevent it laying waste her father's kingdom. As the creature rose from the deep, Perseus pulled out Medusa's head and turned the monster to stone. Perseus and Andromeda, who had fallen in love at first sight, were married soon after.

By the time Perseus returned to Seriphos, Polydectes had made Danae a slave. The king was amazed to see Perseus alive and did not believe he could have killed Medusa. Perseus promptly showed him the Gorgon's head – and he was turned to stone where he stood.

The oracle's prophecy came true, for Perseus did eventually kill his grandfather. He was throwing a discus one day when, by the will of the gods, it hit Acrisius.

The winged horse Pegasus became the steed of another hero, Bellerophon. He rode the horse in his fight against the fire-breathing Chimaera, a monster with a lion's head, a goat's body, and a serpent's tail. Bellerophon killed the creature by thrusting his spear into its throat. The spear had a lump of lead on the end, which the Chimaera's hot breath melted, searing its insides.

Bellerophon was such a great man that he came to think himself the equal of the gods. He rode Pegasus right up to Olympus. But Zeus sent a gadfly to sting the horse, which shied. Bellerophon was flung to earth and ended his days a beggar. As for Pegasus, Zeus used her to carry his thunderbolts.

PEGASUS
The winged horse is shown on this coin from Athens. Bellerophon is supposed to have tamed Pegasus using a bridle given to him by Athena, goddess of wisdom.

Mounted on Pegasus, Bellerophon attacks the fearsome, fire-breathing Chimaera

Atlantis, page 170 ➤

BENTEN AND THE SERPENT KING

LUCKY RIDE
This detail from a
Japanese painting shows
Benten riding an ox, an
animal linked with
good fortune.

BENEATH THE SEAS live the serpent peoples. There the dragon king Ryu-wo reigns in a wonderful palace built of coral and crystal. He has a human body, but a serpent adorns his crown, and his followers are serpents, fishes, and monsters of the deep. He is wise and noble, a guardian of the Shinto faith. Many of those who have fallen by chance into the sea, have lived on, transformed, in the court of the dragon king.

At Kamakura on the Pacific coast of Japan, there is a great temple, something like the dragon king's palace, built to commemorate the marriage of the goddess of love, Benten, and a serpent king, who lived in a pond above the beach on Picture Island.

This serpent was terrorizing the villages, and devouring the children for miles around. Benten could not bear to witness such destruction. Therefore she stirred up an earthquake, and hovered above the serpent's lair in the dust clouds. Descending, she called it forth.

Unlike Ryu-wo, this king was ugly and repulsive, with a serpent's scales and a serpent's flicking tongue. At first Benten was filled with loathing. But the serpent king wooed her with soft and tender words until her heart was melted, and – making him promise to mend his savage ways – she married him.

Words alone won Benten, for she is the goddess of eloquent speech, and also of music. She always carries with her a little stringed instrument called a biwa, and sometimes she will appear in person to great musicians, when they play with all their soul.

Benten wears long, many-coloured robes, and a jewel in her crown, and she is worshipped at beautiful spots all along the sea coast. It is to her that

*Benten agrees to marry the
serpent god if he will end
his reign of terror*

people pray when they are in need of money, for she will give wealth to those who win her favour with well-argued pleas.

THE PHOENIX

THE PHOENIX IS BORN in the sun. Its plumage blends all colours and its call is a sweet harmony of five notes. It bathes only in the purest water that flows from the K'un-lun mountains and it passes the night in the cave of Tan. It can raise its beautiful tail higher than a tall man's head, and wherever it goes the three hundred and sixty varieties of bird gather to pay homage.

Like the other spiritual animals, the dragon, the unicorn, and the turtle, the phoenix contains all things, both male and female, Yin and Yang. Its head is the rooster of the sun, and its back the curve of the crescent moon. Its wings are of the wind, its tailfeathers are the trees and flowers, and its feet are the earth. Whenever a phoenix appears, it is an omen of prosperity. But when it leaves, bad luck will surely follow.

The body of the phoenix contains all things

The three other spiritual animals recognized by the Chinese are the dragon, the unicorn and the turtle

❖

FROM THE ASHES
The Egyptians also believed in a bird called the phoenix, of which there was only ever one. When it grew old, the phoenix built itself a nest of cassia twigs and frankincense and burst into flames. From the heart of this fire, the phoenix was reborn. The ancient Greeks shared this belief.

BIRD OF HARMONY
In Chinese myth, the fabulous phoenix (shown here with a fairy in a 15th-century painting on silk), represented beauty and harmony. For this reason, the phoenix was especially associated with weddings.

VISIONS OF THE END

Every human being foresees an end to his or her life, and all mythologies foresee an end to the world as we know it. Often, as in Norse or Iranian myth, we are told that a new world will arise, purged and purified, from the destruction of this one. Some traditions even look forward to this day of judgement, seeing it not as an end but as a new beginning.

But at the same time, we value our life in the here and now. The mythologies of the world are full of brave men and women who descend into the depths of the dread underworld in search of immortality, advice or – in heartbreaking stories such as *Orpheus and Eurydice* – of loved ones they have lost. Many stories are told, too, of heroes for whom death is not a final end, but merely an interval before they return once more to champion humankind.

Two old men, close to death, meet up after wasting their lives journeying around the world in How Big the World Is!

AENEAS IN THE UNDERWORLD

VENUS
As set down in the
Aeneid by Virgil,
Aeneas's mother was
Venus, Roman goddess
of love and beauty. The
head above is of the
famous statue called
the Venus de Milo.

TO THE UNDERWORLD
This fresco (wall
painting) shows a soul
being escorted to the
Underworld between
two attendants. The
Romans believed that a
soul was taken by spirits
at the moment of death.

AENEAS, SON OF THE goddess Venus and the humble Trojan shepherd Anchises, is famed as the father of the Romans. He became one of the greatest warriors of the city of Troy, which was besieged by the Greeks for many years. When at last the Greeks captured the city, he escaped, carrying his father on his back. After long wanderings, he finally reached Italy.

On the way, Aeneas had many adventures. His father, Anchises, died; he loved and lost Queen Dido of Carthage. But always the will of the gods, and his own great destiny, drove him on.

It happened that, on his journey, Aeneas and his ships arrived at Cumae where the Sibyl lived in her cave, speaking the prophecies of the god Apollo in a voice that echoed and boomed through a hundred mouths in the rock. The temple of Apollo at Cumae had been founded by Daedalus, at the spot where he had landed after his flight from Crete. It was Daedalus himself who had wrought the golden doors of the temple, which captured every scene of the story of King Minos, Queen Pasiphae, and the Minotaur. Every scene that is, except one. Twice Daedalus tried to show the fall of his son Icarus, but his hands trembled too much for the task.

Aeneas approached the Sibyl, and she answered his questions about his future. Then he asked, "Is it true that the gate to the Underworld is here? For I wish to look once more upon the face of my father."

The Sibyl replied, "The door to the Underworld is always open and it is easy to pass through it. But to return: that is hard. If you must go, pluck a golden bough from the sacred grove to take as an offering to Proserpina, Queen of the Underworld. I will guide you."

Aeneas plucked the bough, and it gave a glimmering light as they plunged down into the black hole from which the poisonous breath of the Underworld escaped to heaven. Charon, the grim ferryman, took them across the River Styx, which encircled the Underworld.

In the dark realms, Aeneas saw many that he knew – even Dido, his love, but she would not speak to him. He passed the damned enduring punishments in Tartarus and at last came to the blessed meadows of Elysium. There, he found his father's shade.

"Father," cried Aeneas, "let me embrace you." But when he put his arms around Anchises, it was like trying to hold mist.

◄ *The Fall of Icarus, page 112*

Near them, Aeneas saw many souls eagerly drinking the waters of forgetfulness from the River Lethe. "Why do souls wish to forget this beautiful place and return to the strife of the world?" he asked.

Anchises replied, "In the beginning, all was pure spirit. Some of that spirit burns in the body of each person. But we are bound to life, compelled by love and fear. Only a few souls desire to remain in these fields until the circle of time is completed, when we will all become pure spirit once more. Most souls hunger, sooner or later, for the open sky, and come to drink forgetfulness, and be born again."

Anchises then showed Aeneas a glorious sight: the noble race that would be his descendants. Anchises said that they would be called the Romans and that they would create a great empire that would last for hundreds of years.

At last father and son had to part. Aeneas and the Sibyl made their way back to the land of the living, Aeneas pondering the magnificent destiny the gods had decreed for him.

As Troy burns, Aeneas flees with his father on his back

The Sibyl tells Aeneas to take a golden bough to Proserpina, Queen of the Underworld

The Sibyl looks on as Aeneas tries to embrace the ghost of his father, Anchises

Souls longing to be reborn drink from the River Lethe

THE DEATH OF KING ARTHUR

*Guinevere is rescued by
her lover, Sir Lancelot*

AFTER THE QUEST OF THE HOLY GRAIL, King Arthur and the Knights of the Round Table, who had touched the heart of this world's mystery, were left to live once again in the world of everyday. They continued to uphold right and justice, and to go on quests and take part in jousts and feasts, but somehow the savour was gone from life. Petty squabbles arose and a faction grew up at court that sneered at the lofty aims of the Round Table. Its leader was King Arthur's own son, Mordred. Worst of all, the love between Sir Lancelot and Arthur's wife, Queen Guinevere, became obvious to all. Because of it, the fellowship of the Round Table was broken for ever.

King Arthur

*Arthur's knights ride out
to fight Mordred's army*

❖

THE LAST BATTLE
The site of the battle of Camlann is a mystery. Sources place it in Wales, in Scotland, and on Salisbury Plain in England. One of the most likely sites, however, is Slaughter Bridge, near Camelford in Cornwall, southwest England. Legend has it that the fighting was so fierce the River Camel ran red with blood.

For loving Sir Lancelot, the queen was condemned to be burned at the stake. Lancelot rescued her, but in doing so he killed Sir Gareth and Sir Gaheris, two of the kindest and bravest of all the knights. King Arthur and Sir Gawain, brother of Gareth and Gaheris, declared war on Sir Lancelot to avenge the deaths. The Knights of the Round Table were forced to take sides, friend against friend, in a bitter, futile struggle. And while they were fighting each other, the evil Mordred seized the throne of England and declared himself king.

King Arthur's army faced Mordred's at Camlann. The two sides had just agreed peace when a knight saw an adder in the grass, and struck at the snake with his sword. The sun flashed on the drawn blade, and both armies, suspecting treachery, fell upon each other.

◄ *The Holy Grail, page 89*

That was the grimmest, bloodiest battle ever fought, a nightmare of shrieking steel and dying men.

Near the end, King Arthur looked around him, and saw that of all his host of knights, only two, Sir Lucan and Sir Bedivere, were still alive, and they were sorely wounded.

"Alas," said King Arthur, "that ever I should see this doleful day. For now I have come to my end."

Then Arthur saw Sir Mordred, leaning on his sword by a heap of dead men. "Give me my spear," said the king to Sir Lucan. "There is the traitor who has brought us to this."

"Let him be," said Sir Lucan. "He is in anguish."

But Arthur challenged Mordred and ran him through with his spear. And when Mordred felt his death blow, he hauled himself bodily up the spear to strike his father down with his sword. Sir Mordred fell dead, and Arthur swooned away.

LOVERS' MEETING
This illustration from a 15th-century French manuscript shows Lancelot and Guinevere's first kiss. Their meeting has been arranged by a courtier called Galleot, who looks on.

Mordred

The wounded king commands Sir Bedivere to throw his sword into the lake

Sir Bedivere

Arthur

Sir Lucan

Sir Lucan and Sir Bedivere carried the wounded king from the field of battle. They took him to the lakeside where, when he was young, Arthur had received his magic sword, Excalibur, from the Lady of the Lake. The effort was too much for Sir Lucan, and he too died.

Then the king told Sir Bedivere, "Take my sword, and throw it in the lake. Then come back and tell me what you saw."

Sir Bedivere took the sword. But, thinking that no good could possibly come from throwing away such a valuable blade, he did not cast the sword into the lake as the king had ordered.

THE ISLE OF AVALON
Glastonbury Tor in Somerset, southwest England, is believed to be the Isle of Avalon where Arthur was buried after the battle of Camlann. It was once surrounded by marshes and deep pools.

*Sir Bedivere, the last of Arthur's knights, waves
a sad farewell as the dying king is borne away*

"What did you see?" asked King Arthur on his return.
"Sire," Sir Bedivere answered uncertainly, "I saw
nothing but waves and winds."

"Go back," said the king sadly, "and do as I asked."

Sir Bedivere returned to the lakeside, and this time threw the
sword as far as he could into the lake. To his amazement, an arm
appeared from under the water, caught the blade, and brandished it
three times, before sinking beneath the water.

Sir Bedivere told the king what he had seen.

"Then my end is truly come," whispered King Arthur. "Now take
me to the shore."

Sir Bedivere took the king upon his back and staggered to the
water's edge. A barge appeared, with three ladies sitting in it, one of
whom was King Arthur's half-sister, the witch Queen Morgan le Fay.
She said, "Ah, dear brother, why have you tarried so long?" And she
helped the king into the barge.

Then Sir Bedivere cried, "Lord Arthur, what shall become of me?"

King Arthur replied, "You must look after yourself, for in me there is
no trust to trust in. I am going to the isle of Avalon, to heal me of my
grievous wounds. If you never hear of me again, pray for my soul."

And the barge moved slowly out across the still water, into the grey
mist, and disappeared.

Some say King Arthur died of his terrible wounds. But others say
that he recovered, and lives still in the magical isle of Avalon, waiting
to return at the moment of England's direst need. For on the
monument that was raised to his memory by Sir Bedivere, the
wording reads, "Here lies Arthur, the Once and Future King."

MORT D'ARTHUR
Faithful Sir Bedivere
returns Arthur's sword
to the Lady of the Lake
in this illustration from
a 14th-century French
manuscript. In the
foreground, the wounded
king waits for death.

THE VOYAGE OF BRAN

O NE DAY, AS BRAN, SON OF FEBAL, walked near his fort, he heard sweet, tinkling music in the air. Listening to it, he fell asleep. When he awoke, he found lying beside him a silver apple branch with white blossom on it.

He took the branch and returned home, where his warriors awaited him. There he found a woman who greeted him and sang to him of the joys of the sea and the world beyond, with its many islands, each with its own delights.

"Leave this lazy life," she said, "and take to the sea."

"I will," he replied. With that, the silver apple branch leapt from his hand to hers.

So Bran set to sea, with three companies of nine men, each led by one of his foster brothers. After two days and two nights, they met Manannan, god of the sea, riding over the waves in his chariot – for to him the ocean was as easy to cross as solid earth. Manannan, too, sang to Bran, telling him of the wonders of the deep, and the numberless islands of the sea.

CELTIC BROOCH
Known as the Hunterston brooch, this beautiful piece was made in Ireland around AD 700. Following the destruction of the Roman Empire, Ireland had become an important centre of Christianity, art, and learning. The Celtic myths were first written down by Irish monks.

Bran hearkens to the woman's thrilling songs of voyaging and adventure

Manannan, god of the sea, tells Bran of the wonders of the deep

❖

BRAN THE BLESSED
Welsh legend tells of
another hero called
Bran – Bran the Blessed.
He was killed by a
poisoned arrow while
battling the Irish king
Matholwch. His head was
buried on the White Hill
in London (where the
Tower of London now
stands) as a protection
against invasion. King
Arthur dug it up,
preferring to rely on his
people's valour.

The first island they came to was called the Isle of Joy. All the people on it were smiling and laughing – not at anything in particular, just for the sake of happiness. Bran sent a man ashore to find out what was happening. As soon as the man set foot on the island, he too began to gape and grin, and would not respond to questions from the ship, or return to it. So they left him there, and sailed on.

The next island they came to was the Isle of Women. The chief woman called out, "Welcome, strangers. Come ashore."

For what seemed only a year, Bran and his men stayed in revelry and delight on the Isle of Women. Then, one man began to speak of the green hills of home, and one by one they all began to feel homesick.

*Bran's voyage takes him to the Isle of Joy
and to the Isle of Women*

❖

THE OTHERWORLD
The magical isles Bran
sails to were known as
the Otherworld. They
were believed to lie
somewhere in the west,
across what we now
know as the Atlantic.

Happy as they were, there was nothing for it but to leave.

The women begged them not to go, but their minds were made up. "Whatever you do," said the chief woman, "first pick up your friend from the Isle of Joy. After that, I advise you to carry on your journey. Don't go back."

Bran picked up the man from the Isle of Joy; but the man could not remember what it was he had been smiling at all this time. Then, disregarding the chief woman's advice, they set a homeward course for Ireland.

As they neared the coast, they saw a large gathering of people on the beach. Bran hailed them, declaring that he was Bran, son of Febal, home from his sea-wanderings. The people answered, "We know of no such man."

Then an old man said, "But there is a legend of a man of that name, who set out on a voyage and was lost for ever."

The man who had first grown homesick, impatient with this prattle, leapt from the ship on to the beach. But as soon as his feet touched the ground, his body turned to ashes, like one long dead. For time runs differently in

THE RETURN OF BRAN
This dramatic seascape, looking westwards from the southwest coast of Ireland, may be near the spot where Bran and his men attempted to land after their voyage to the magical isles.

Bran and his crew at last return home, but find that the people have forgotten them

the magical isles, and one year on the Isle of Women was the same as many, many years back home.

Bran related his adventures to the people on the beach, so that the record of his voyage should not be lost, then turned the prow of his ship away from land and sailed away. From that day, no one has set eyes on Bran, son of Febal. But surely he is sailing still, from island to island in the seas beyond the sea.

❖

VOYAGER HEROES
The tale of Bran, the voyager hero, is echoed by other countries' myths and epics, especially the wanderings of the Greek hero Odysseus.

THE DEATH OF BALDER

B ALDER THE BEAUTIFUL, Odin's son, suffered from nightmares. Though by day he knew he was loved by all, night after night he dreamed he was about to be killed.

So Odin mounted his eight-legged steed Sleipnir and rode over the rainbow bridge to Hel in Niflheim, land of the dead. Past the hound of Hel he rode, to the grave of a prophetess, long dead. With his magic he raised her from her sleep, asking, "Why are the halls of Hel prepared as if for a feast, with jewels and gold everywhere?"

She replied, "The mead is brewing for Balder in Hel."

"Who shall slay him, the best of the gods?" asked Odin.

"The blind god Hoder shall strike the blow."

"And who shall grieve for him?"

"You shall, Odin. Ask me no more." And with that, the prophetess sank back into her sleep of death.

The news that Odin brought back from Hel was of no comfort to the gods. Still Balder tossed and turned, dreaming of his own death.

So Balder's mother, Frigg, set out through the world, asking every thing she came across to swear never to hurt Balder. Fire swore. Water swore. The animals and birds swore. The snakes swore. The diseases swore. The earth and the trees swore. The metals swore. The very stones swore never to harm him.

At last, Balder was safe. Soon the gods had a new game to play. Balder would stand still, and each of the gods would hurl some deadly thing at him. They pelted him with rocks, cut at him with swords, and stabbed at him with spears,

Odin rides Sleipnir to the hall of Hel in the land of the dead to find out why his beloved son Balder is tormented by nightmares

SLEIPNIR
This picture stone from Gotland, Sweden, shows Odin's eight-legged stallion, Sleipnir, who was faster than any other horse. The rider may be Odin, or a dead warrior entering Valhalla, Odin's hall.

◄ *Thor in the Land of Giants, page 118*

162

but nothing hurt him at all. He came away without a scratch, and all the gods roared with laughter.

That is, all the gods but one. Sly Loki had no taste for such innocent fun. He took on the guise of an old woman and went to see Frigg. He asked her what all the laughter was about, and Frigg explained how everything in the world had sworn not to hurt Balder. "What, everything in the whole world?" exclaimed Loki. "Everything except that young sprig of mistletoe," said Frigg.

Loki went straight away and plucked the mistletoe, and took it to the assembly of the gods. He approached the blind god, Hoder, and asked, "Why are you not throwing things at Balder?"

"I can't see where he is," said Hoder, "and I have no weapon."

"Why don't you throw this little stick?" said Loki. "I will guide your hand."

So Hoder threw the mistletoe at Balder, and it pierced him, and killed him. And that was the unluckiest deed ever done among gods or men.

The gods' laughter died in their throats. They could not speak or move. They just stared at the golden god, as he lay dead.

No one lifted a hand against Loki, for this was hallowed ground. They let him go. And then their tears burst out of them, in terrible sobs.

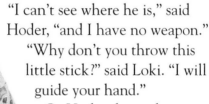

As Loki guides Hoder's hand to throw the deadly mistletoe, the other gods pelt Balder with sticks and stones, knowing they cannot harm him

MISTLETOE

This evergreen plant with soft, sticky, white berries grows high up in broad-leaved trees, particularly old apple trees. For centuries it has been associated with superstitions and customs. In ancient Scandinavia, mistletoe hanging outside a house meant a welcome within – it was the plant of peace.

They built Balder's funeral pyre on his great ship, and launched it with the help of the giantess Hyrrokkin. All the gods were there when Odin bent to whisper his last farewell into Balder's ear. Odin slid his gold ring, Draupnir, on to Balder's arm. Then he lit the pyre, and sent Balder on his long journey.

FRIGG
The fertility goddess
Frigg was the wife of
Odin and mother of all
the gods. She had an
unfortunate gift: she
could see into the
future, but could do
nothing to change it.
Frigg was also the
goddess of marriage and
so her day, Friday, was a
lucky day for weddings.

SILVER ARM RING
This solid silver Viking
bracelet, found in Fyn
in Denmark, would
have been worn on the
upper arm. Armlets
such as this were prized
possesssions, often given
by a king to a brave
warrior. Odin's gold arm
ring, Draupnir, was one
of the three treasures of
the gods.

Frigg asked, "Is there any one among the
gods who will ride to Hel, and bargain
with Hel to let Balder come back to us?"
And Hermod, another of Odin's sons,
leaped on Sleipnir and set off for Hel. He
rode through dark valleys, until he came
to the gates of Hel. He begged to be let
in, and there he found his brother Balder.

Hermod pleaded with the goddess Hel
to let his brother return with him to the
land of the living. "Everyone loves
Balder. Everyone weeps for him," he said.

"If it is as you say," said Hel, "Balder
may return to life. But everything in the
world must weep for him. If one refuses, he must stay with me."
Hermod took leave of his brother, who gave him back the arm ring
Draupnir as a token for his father, Odin. Forever afterwards, on every
ninth night, Draupnir has wept, and its tears always form eight more
arm rings of the same size.

Frigg went once again through the world, and everything that had
sworn not to harm Balder wept for him. Even the mistletoe that killed
him wept for him. But at last she came to a cave with a giantess
sitting in it. And the giantess told her, "I will weep no tears for Balder.
I had no use for him, alive or dead. Let Hel keep what she has." For
the giantess was Loki in disguise, and Loki would not weep.

The gods had tolerated Loki's mischief-making, but this time
he had gone too far. Loki fled from their fury to a house on
a mountain. The house had doors facing in every
direction so he could see anyone coming. By day he
hid under a waterfall, in the form of a salmon.

*Hermod begs Hel to let Balder
return to the land of the living*

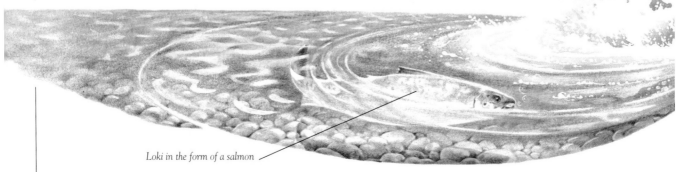

Loki in the form of a salmon

Sitting in his house one night, Loki began to wonder if the gods might catch him, even in his salmon form. Idly he wove a net and tossed it into the fire. Suddenly he saw the gods approaching, and fled to the safety of his waterfall.

The gods entered the house, looked into the fire, and saw the net. Realizing that Loki must be disguised as a fish, they made a new net to the pattern Loki himself had devised.

They caught Loki, carried him to a cave, and bound him across three stones, tied down with the entrails of one of his own sons.

Loki's mountaintop hideout

Odin

LOKI THE TRICKSTER
Loki was a mischievous spirit of air and fire, who could be malicious. His nickname, "the shape-changer", referred to his ability to change his shape when he wanted to trick or deceive the other gods . On the stone bellows-shield above, Loki is depicted with his lips sewn together. This refers to another story about Loki, in which a dwarf sews up his lips to stop him from talking.

The gods realize that Loki is hiding under the waterfall, disguised as a fish, and so they make a new net to catch him

There they left him, with a serpent hanging above him, dripping venom on to his face.

His faithful wife, Sigyn, still sits beside him, catching the venom in a cup. But every so often, the cup becomes full, she turns away to empty it, and the poison drops on to Loki's face. As he writhes in agony, the earth shakes.

Thus was the death of Balder, Odin and Frigg's favourite son, avenged. But it is said that, one day, after Ragnarok, twilight of the gods, he will return to life again.

Loki's wife tries to catch the serpent's venom in a cup before it drips on to his face

Ragnarok, page 174 ➤

ORPHEUS AND EURYDICE

THE MUSIC OF ORPHEUS
Dating from the 3rd
century AD, this mosaic
comes from Antioch in
Turkey, formerly a Syrian
city. It shows Orpheus
playing to the birds and
beasts. Orpheus was the
son of Calliope, chief of
the Nine Muses,
daughters of Zeus who
inspired music, poetry,
and drama.

ORPHEUS, THE SON OF the muse Calliope, was the most gifted musician who ever lived. When he played his lyre, birds stopped in their flight to listen and wild animals lost their fear. The trees would bend to catch his tunes on the wind. He was given his lyre by Apollo; some say Apollo was his father.

Orpheus was married to Eurydice. Now Eurydice was so lovely that she attracted a man named Aristaeus. When she refused his advances, he chased her. Fleeing him, she trod on a serpent, which bit her, and she died.

Orpheus was beside himself with sorrow. Taking up his lyre he travelled to the Underworld to try to win her back. The plaintive, weeping song of his lyre charmed the ferryman, Charon, into carrying him alive over the dread River Styx. The lyre's lullaby sent Cerberus, the three-headed watchdog of the gates, to sleep; its caressing call relieved the torments of the damned.

Finally Orpheus came before the throne of Hades himself. The king of the dead was annoyed that a living man had entered his realm, but the agony in Orpheus's music moved him, and he wept iron tears. His wife, Persephone, begged him to listen to Orpheus's plea.

Orpheus

Persephone

Hades

Eurydice

Cerberus

*Persephone begs her husband to help Orpheus, whose
mournful playing and singing has moved Hades to tears*

So Hades granted his wish. Eurydice could follow Orpheus to the upper world. But only on one condition: that he did not look at her until she once more walked under the sun.

So Orpheus set off on his journey up the steep track that led out of death's dark kingdom, playing tunes of joy and celebration as he walked, to guide the shade of Eurydice back to life. He never once looked back, until he reached the sunlight. But then he turned, to make sure Eurydice was still there.

For a moment he saw her, nearly at the entrance to the dark tunnel, nearly alive again. But as he looked, she frayed once more into a thin ghost, her final cry of love and grief no more than a whisper on the breeze from hell. He had lost her for ever.

In black despair, Orpheus became bitter. He refused to look at any woman, hating to be reminded of the loss of his beloved Eurydice. Furious at being scorned by him, a group of wild women called the Maenads set upon him in a frenzy and tore him limb from limb. They cast his severed head into the River Hebrus, and it floated away, still singing, "Eurydice! Eurydice!"

Weeping, the Nine Muses gathered up his limbs and buried them by Mount Olympus. It is said that from that day onwards, the nightingales that live nearby always sing more sweetly than any others. For Orpheus, in death, was reunited with his beloved Eurydice.

As for the Maenads who had so cruelly murdered Orpheus, the gods did not grant them the mercy of death. Even as they stamped their feet on the earth in triumph, they felt their toes lengthen and curl into the ground. The more they struggled, the more deeply rooted they became. Their legs became wooden and heavy, and so on up their bodies, until they were changed completely into mute oak trees. And there they stood through the years, battered by the angry winds that once had thrilled to the sound of Orpheus's lyre, until at last their dead, hollow trunks toppled to the ground.

NIGHTINGALE
This small, rather ordinary-looking bird has a rich melodious song, hence the compliment "she sings like a nightingale".

The gods turn Orpheus's murderers, the Maenads, into oak trees

❖

THE MAENADS
These female followers of Dionysus, god of wine and pleasure, roamed mountainsides, playing flutes, banging tambourines, and dancing themselves into a frenzy. In this wild state the Maenads were capable of killing with their bare hands.

SEDNA

SPIRIT MASK
In Inuit myth, several spirits influence the forces of nature. This wooden mask contains references to a number of spirits. It moves in a different way as the wearer moves – showing how interlinked the nature spirits are.

SEDNA IS KNOWN as the Mother of Sea Beasts. Once she was a human girl, but now she is a goddess who lives at the bottom of the sea. This is how it happened.

Sedna did not want to get married. She rejected all the young men of her village. But then she fell in love with a dog, and married him.

"This will bring bad luck," said the rejected young men, who had all wanted Sedna for themselves. So they took her out to sea in a boat, and pushed her overboard. Sedna clung to the side of the boat, but they chopped off her fingers. As the fingers fell into the sea, they turned into the first seals, and other sea creatures. Sedna sank to the bottom of the sea, where she became ruler of the Underworld, mistress of all living things.

Because of the cruel fate she suffered, Sedna is quick to anger. When anyone offends her, she shuts away all the beasts, so that men cannot fish or hunt.

Then some daring man with the special powers of a shaman, a priest who can communicate with the spirits, must make a perilous descent under the sea, to soothe her. He must venture past the terrible guardians of Sedna's house, which include a big fierce black dog, until he reaches Sedna herself.

Now, the sins of mankind fall down through the water and collect in Sedna's hair as grease and grime. But because she has no fingers, she cannot do anything about it. So the shaman must dress Sedna's filthy hair into two thick braids, untangling its knots and picking out the dirt. In gratitude, Sedna frees the beasts, and mankind can eat again.

As Sedna sinks to the bottom of the sea, her severed fingers turn into the first sea creatures

Sedna's fingers become seals and walruses, whales and dolphins

HOW BIG THE WORLD IS!

The two couples set off in opposite directions with their dog sledges

SEALSKIN PAINTING
In the Arctic lands, the Inuit people are dependent on hunting and fishing for food. The pictures on this painting show people riding in sledges drawn by reindeer, paddling in canoes, and harpooning seals, a valuable source of meat and skins.

TWO COUPLES lived together. One day, the two men fell to talking. "The world is big," said the first.

"How big?" wondered the second.

"Let's find out," answered the first.

So they took their sledges and set off in opposite directions. Their wives cried at parting from each other, but each accompanied her husband, running beside his sledge.

Year after year they travelled. The wives had babies, and the babies grew up. Then they had children, and so on, until there were two whole tribes travelling across the ice.

The original couples grew old and frail. The men could no longer drive their sledges; the women could no longer keep up the pace beside them. But still they travelled.

At last, each of them saw movement in the far distance. They kept on going, and, finally, they met, back where they had started.

"The world is big," said the first man.

"Even bigger than we thought," answered the second. And then they died.

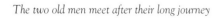

The two old men meet after their long journey

ATLANTIS

T HE GREEKS HAD many legends of the distant past: of Phoroneus, the first man, and of Deucalion and Pyrrha, who survived a flood sent by Zeus to rid the world of evil men. But when the Greek statesman Solon related these tales to the priests of ancient Egypt, they laughed. "You Greeks know nothing of your own history. You talk of one flood, but there have been many. It was in such a flood that your ancestors perished!" And the priests told Solon the story of the island of Atlantis, from where, nine thousand years before, the noblest race of men that ever lived ruled most of the known world.

A poor couple named Evenor and Leucippe once lived on a rocky island with their daughter, Clito. Poseidon, god of the sea, was smitten by Clito's beauty and married her. He then reshaped the island to make it a dwelling fit for his new bride.

He fashioned it into a series of circular belts of sea and land, with an island at the centre that basked in sun and beauty. The rich plains brought forth wheat, fruit, and vegetables in abundance, the forested hills sustained all kinds of animals – even herds of elephants – and beneath the soil were many precious ores.

Clito bore Poseidon five sets of twin boys. They were all kings, and the oldest, Atlas, was the high king, and his sons after him. The beautiful kingdom came to be called Atlantis.

SHADES OF ATLANTIS
Ancient ruins lying
beneath the waters of
a mountain pool in
Pamukkale, Turkey,
bear witness to quick-
tempered Poseidon's
destructive power.

*The beautiful kingdom of Atlantis is a series
of belts of land connected by bridges*

The people of Atlantis were wise in the arts of peace and war and soon ruled all the peoples of the Mediterranean. All of the island's kings added to the country's store of riches. The outer wall of the city of Atlantis was coated with brass, and its inner one with tin. The palace at the centre, with Poseidon's temple, was covered in gold. The buildings were built of white, black, and red stones: sometimes all one colour, sometimes in intricate patterns. A great harbour was opened up to the sea, and bridges were built between the belts of land.

Thus was Atlantis, in the days of its greatness.

For many years, the ten kings ruled wisely and well, each passing on his wisdom to his heir. But as generation succeeded generation, the kings' divine blood grew thinner and they fell more and more under the sway of mortal passions and worldly desires. Where once they had valued precious things simply for their beauty, they now fell prey to greed. Where once the people had lived

Poseidon stirs up a tidal wave to engulf the city of Atlantis

together in friendship and harmony, they now squabbled over power and glory. Great Zeus, seeing this favoured race descend day by day into the pit of human ambitions and vices, rebuked Poseidon for allowing such a thing to happen. And Poseidon, in sorrow and anger, stirred up the sea. A huge tidal wave engulfed Atlantis and the island sank for ever beneath the waters.

Where it lies, no one knows for certain – nor whether, under the ocean, Poseidon's children once more walk the streets of Atlantis in peace and wisdom, or if only the fishes play among the sea-worn bones of this fabled city.

The great city of Atlantis lies beneath the waves

❖

THE REAL ATLANTIS? Archaeologists believe Atlantis may have been the island of Stronghyle (Santorini) in the eastern Mediterranean. Around 1500 BC, a volcanic eruption submerged the island.

THE DEATH OF PAN

PAN'S PIPE
Pan was famous for playing reed pipes. This is the reed he might have used: *Arundo donax*, or Spanish reed. It has been used as a pipe instrument for 5,000 years.

P AN, GOD OF HUNTERS, shepherds, and all wild things, was one of the strangest of all Greek gods. He had two little horns like a goat, a goat's hairy legs, and delicate goat's hooves. He haunted lonely, wild places, playing tunes on a set of pipes made from reeds. He played reed pipes because the nymph Syrinx, with whom he had fallen in love, had escaped him by begging the gods to turn her into a reed.

Pan was worshipped by the Egyptians as well as the Greeks. Those who felt his presence were often seized with a terrible fear, and fled, in what we now call a panic. Some people say his presence can still be felt in lonely spots. However, a strange story is told that, during the reign of the Roman Emperor Tiberius, between AD 14 and 37 , a ship sailing to Italy past the Greek island of Paxoi was hailed by a godlike voice saying, "The great god Pan is dead!"

Pan haunts lonely country places. Panic grips those that sense his presence

Sailors on a ship spread the news of Pan's death

The sailors on board ship repeated the cry whenever they saw land, shouting out to anyone with ears to hear: "The great god Pan is dead!" And a terrible weeping rose up from the empty countryside.

THE RAINBOW SERPENT

THE WORLD WAS CREATED by Nana-Buluku, the one god, who is neither male nor female. In time, Nana-Buluku gave birth to twins, Mawu and Lisa, and it is they who shaped the world and control it still, with their fourteen children, the Vodu, the lesser gods.

Mawu is the moon. She lives in the west and the night-time is her time. Lisa is the sun; he lives in the east and the daytime is his time.

In the beginning, before Mawu had any children, the rainbow serpent Aido-Hwedo already existed – created to serve Nana-Buluku. The creator was carried everywhere in Aido-Hwedo's mouth. Rivers, mountains, and valleys twine and curve because that is how the rainbow serpent Aido-Hwedo moves.

Wherever they stopped for the night, mountains arose, formed from the serpent's dung. That is why if you dig down deep into a mountain, you find riches.

Now when Nana-Buluku had finished his work, he realized that the earth just couldn't carry everything that he had created – all the mountains, trees, people, and animals. So, to keep the earth from capsizing, the creator asked Aido-Hwedo to coil beneath it, to cushion the earth – like the pad people wear on their heads when carrying a heavy burden.

Because Aido-Hwedo cannot stand heat, the creator made the ocean for the serpent to live in. And there Aido-Hwedo has remained since the beginning of time, with his tail in his mouth. Even though the water keeps Aido-Hwedo cool, he sometimes shifts about trying to get comfortable, and that's what causes earthquakes.

Nana-Buluku charged the red monkeys that live beneath the sea to keep Aido-Hwedo fed, and they spend their time forging the iron bars that are the serpent's food. But sooner or later the monkeys' supply of iron is bound to run out and then Aido-Hwedo will have nothing to eat. Famished with hunger he will start to chew his own tail and then his writhings and convulsions will be so terrible that the whole earth will tilt, overburdened as it is with people and things.

The earth will slip into the sea, and that will be that!

Mawu, the moon

Nana-Buluku, the creator, rides in the serpent's mouth

Lisa, the sun

Red monkeys living under the sea forge iron bars for the rainbow serpent to eat

RAGNAROK

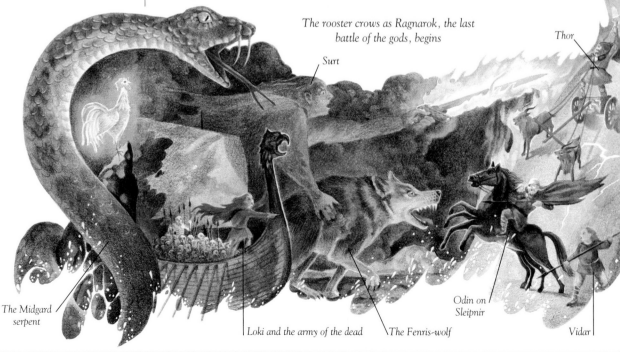

THE GOLDEN ROOSTER crows to wake the gods to each bright morning. But there will come a last twilight of the gods. It will be an axe-age, a sword-age, a wind-age, a wolf-age. This is Ragnarok, when all will be brought to wreck.

Brother will fight brother; all barriers will fall.

The Fenris-wolf will break free from his fetters; Loki the trickster will sail to the world's ruin with an army of the dead, in a ship made of dead men's nails. A bitter winter it will be.

Surt, who has waited at the entrance to Muspell with a blazing sword since the beginning of time, will go to war against the gods, and all nine worlds will be seared with his flames. At his side will come the Fenris-wolf, its jaws agape. The Midgard serpent will spew poison over land and sea.

Then Heimdall the watcher will blow his horn, and the gods will ride to battle, in glorious array. Thor will destroy the Midgard serpent, but when he steps back nine paces from it, he will fall down dead from its poison. The wolf will swallow Odin, the All-Father; Odin's son Vidar will rend the wolf apart in vengeance. Heimdall and Loki will destroy each other.

VIKING SWORD
The Viking, or Norse, warrior's favourite weapon was his sword. Odin, the Norse god of victory in battle, had a magic sword, which was sometimes called "Odin's flame".

The rooster crows as Ragnarok, the last battle of the gods, begins

Surt

Thor

The Midgard serpent

Loki and the army of the dead

The Fenris-wolf

Odin on Sleipnir

Vidar

◄ *The Death of Balder, page 162*

The earth will sink into the sea. The sun will turn black. The bright stars will fall from the heavens. The very sky will burn.

Death will come to the gods, to the giants, to the elves and dwarfs, to men and women, the sons and daughters of Ask and Embla.

But two will be saved, hidden by Yggdrasil, the world tree. Lif and Lifthrasir are their names. The morning dew will be their meat and drink, and from them mankind will be reborn.

Earth will rise a second time, fair and green.

Odin's sons Balder and Hoder will return to life. The rivers will fill with fish, and the fields with corn.

THE DEATH OF ODIN
This detail from the Ragnarok Stone shows Odin, with a raven on his shoulder – either Huginn or Munnin – being swallowed by the Fenris-wolf. Carved by a Viking sculptor, the stone is at Kirk Andreas on the Isle of Man.

Heimdall

Death and destruction come to all on earth, except for Lif and Lifthrasir

Lifthrasir

Lif

Balder

And walking the meadows of the risen earth, talking in wonder of what was and will be, the children of Lif and Lifthrasir shall find in the grass the gold chessboards on which the gods played out their games, and remember Odin, the High One, the All-Father, and his children in their glory, in the golden halls of Asgard.

Balder and Hoder come back to life

Hoder

THE PURIFYING STREAM

Gayomart leads the faithful over the Cinvat Bridge

Mashya and Mashyoi

Gayomart

The Cinvat Bridge

Mashya and Mashyoi

Gayomart

Wise Ahura Mazda listens patiently as the evil Ahriman begs for mercy

Ahura Mazda

Ahriman

Saoshyant

A
S TIME NEARS its end, Saoshyant, the saviour, will come to prepare the world to be made anew and help Ahura Mazda, the one who knows, destroy the evil Ahriman. Mashya and Mashyoi, the first humans, first drank water, then ate plants, then milk, then meat. In the time of Saoshyant, people will cease to need food, giving up first meat, then milk, then plants, then water, until finally they need nothing.

JUDGES OF SOULS
In Iranian myth, three judges, Rashnu, Mithra and Saosha, judge the dead. The good go to heaven, but the bad are sent down into hell, called Druj.

There will be no more sin and self-indulgence, so Az, the demon of lust, created by Ahriman, will be starved of the sensations on which she has glutted. She will turn to her creator, and seek to swallow him up. Ahriman will beg Ahura Mazda, the wise, the all-knowing, to save him, and Ahura Mazda will cast him from creation through the very hole Ahriman made when he broke in.

Then time will come to an end, and there will be a new start for the world. Saoshyant will raise the dead, and Ahura Mazda will marry body to soul. First to rise will be Gayomart, the first fire-priest; then Mashya and Mashyoi, our mother and father; then the rest of humanity. They will come back across the Cinvat Bridge from the joys of heaven or the horrors of hell, wherever their acts and their consciences have sent them. Even those who have killed a dog will come, although – because dogs go out at night to battle the creatures of the evil spirit – anyone who kills a dog kills his own soul for nine generations, and cannot cross the Cinvat Bridge until he atones for his sin. That bridge is wide for the faithful, but it is narrow as a needle for the sinner.

All the metal in the mountains of the world will melt, and each man and woman will pass though the stream of molten metal and emerge purified.

Those who were faithful to Ahura Mazda and lived a holy, creative, generous, productive life will feel that they are walking through warm milk. However those who were seduced by Ahriman will suffer terrible agony as all their sins are burned away.

The new world will be immortal and everlasting. Those who lived to adulthood will be brought back to life at the age of forty; those who died as children will be brought back at fifteen; all will live happily with their family and friends.

CULT OF FIRE
This Persian coin from the 4th century AD shows a sacrifice being made by fire-worshippers. Fire is the symbol of Ahura Mazda, the supreme god. In Ahura Mazda's temples, fire-priests always keep a flame burning as a sign of the god's presence.

Those that have lived good lives bathe happily in the stream of molten metal, but those that have lived bad lives suffer agony

RUGGED ROCKS
The landscape of Iran provides a suitable setting for this story, in which molten metal pours down mountains to cleanse the world.

GODS AND PANTHEONS

The mythologies of the world contain gods and goddesses of every description: supreme beings who create the world, minor deities only associated with a particular place or thing, gods of the underworld, sun gods and sea gods, gods of war, gods of music, gods of farming, trickster gods and gods of love.

These wonderful beings may be worshipped by a great empire or just a single village.

Gods and Pantheons contains a brief who's who of all the major mythological figures – the gods, the goddesses, the heroes, and the monsters – that appear in this book. This section also provides a simplified guide to the pantheons of Greek and Norse mythology.

This stone from the island of Gotland, Sweden shows Odin arriving in Valhalla, riding on his horse, Sleipnir. A Valkyrie holds out a drinking horn in welcome

WHO'S WHO IN MYTHOLOGY

Athena, goddess of wisdom

AENEAS (in-**ee**-us)
❖ *Roman*

Aeneas, the son of Anchises and the goddess Venus, was a prince of Troy. When the Greek army captured the city of Troy at the end of the long Trojan War, they allowed Aeneas to take with him whatever he valued most: he chose his aged father, Anchises. After a long voyage, during which Aeneas fell in love with, then abandoned, Dido, Queen of Carthage, Aeneas landed in Italy; the Roman emperors claimed descent from him. His story is told in the *Aeneid*, an epic poem written between 29 and 19 BC by the Roman poet Virgil.

AHRIMAN (**ah**-ri-mun)
❖ *Iranian*

In the Zoroastrian religion, Ahriman is the god of darkness and evil and the bitter foe of the lord of light, Ahura Mazda. Ahriman sent down death and disease to bring misery to human beings and to spoil the earthly paradise that Ahura Mazda created.

AHURA MAZDA (**ah**-hoor-a **maz**-da)
❖ *Iranian*

Ahura Mazda became the focus of a one-god religion founded by the prophet Zoroaster around 600 BC. The god represents light and truth; his enemy is Ahriman. A flame, symbolizing Ahura Mazda's presence, is always kept burning in the god's temples.

AIOINA (eye-**oy**-na)
❖ *Japan, Ainu*

Aioina is the divine man sent down to this, the floating world, by the supreme god Kamui to teach the Ainu, the first inhabitants of Japan, how to hunt and cook. Some say that Aioina actually made the Ainu; the word Ainu means "men".

AMATERASU (**ah**-ma-tay-**rah**-soo)
❖ *Japanese*

Amaterasu is the Shinto goddess of the sun. The chief story about her centres on the sun's crucial role in the earth's fertility. When Amaterasu hid her face in a cave, the crops withered. Only when she was lured out by the other gods did the world revive.

ANU (**ah**-noo)
❖ *Sumerian*

Anu, or An, is the supreme god of Sumerian mythology and the father of Enlil, the god of earth and air. He is associated with the heavens and his sign is a star.

ANUBIS (a-**nyoo**-bis)
❖ *Egyptian*

The son of Osiris and a goddess of the dead, Nepthys, Anubis is the jackal-headed god of the dead. He guides the souls of those who have recently died to Osiris, ruler of the Underworld, for judgement. Anubis is the lord of embalming and guardian of tombs.

APHRODITE (aff-ro-**die**-tee)
❖ *Greek*
VENUS (**vee**-nus)
❖ *Roman*

The daughter of the Titan Uranus, Aphrodite is the Greek goddess of love (she was known as Venus to the Romans). Although married to Hephaestus, the lame god of fire and metalwork, she had many love affairs, notably with the god of war, Ares. Her other loves included the beautiful boy Adonis, and the humble herdsman Anchises, father of the Roman hero Aeneas.

APOLLO (a-**poll**-oh)
❖ *Greek*

The god of healing, poetry, music, and light, Apollo is also identified with the movement of the sun. The god's shrine at Delphi was the home of the oracle, through whose prophecies Apollo revealed the future to mortals. Apollo is the son of Zeus and the Titaness Leto and the twin brother of Artemis. The brilliant musician Orpheus was one of his sons.

ANUBIS (a-**nyoo**-bis)

ARES (**air**-eez)
❖ *Greek*
MARS (**marz**)
❖ *Roman*

The son of Zeus and Hera, Ares is the god of war, a bloodthirsty fighter highly disliked by the other gods on Olympus – except for Aphrodite. Mars, the Roman god of war, was a more important and noble figure, and was regarded as the father of Romulus, founder of Rome.

ARTEMIS (**ar**-tem-iss)
❖ *Greek*
DIANA (die-**an**-a)
❖ *Roman*

Artemis, the goddess of hunting, is the beautiful twin sister of Apollo. She is the protector of all young girls. If offended, she has a fierce temper. When a hunter, Actaeon, accidentally caught sight of her bathing naked in a river, she turned him into a stag and he was caught and torn to pieces by his own dogs.

ARTHUR (**ar**-thur)
❖ *Celtic*

Presiding over his court at Camelot with his queen, Guinevere, King Arthur is the central figure in a mass of medieval literature, much of it French. These tales tell of the deeds of his Knights of the Round Table, who included Lancelot, Gawain, and Galahad. In real life, Arthur may have been a Celtic chieftain who resisted the invading Saxons in southwest England around AD 500 .

THE GREEK PANTHEON

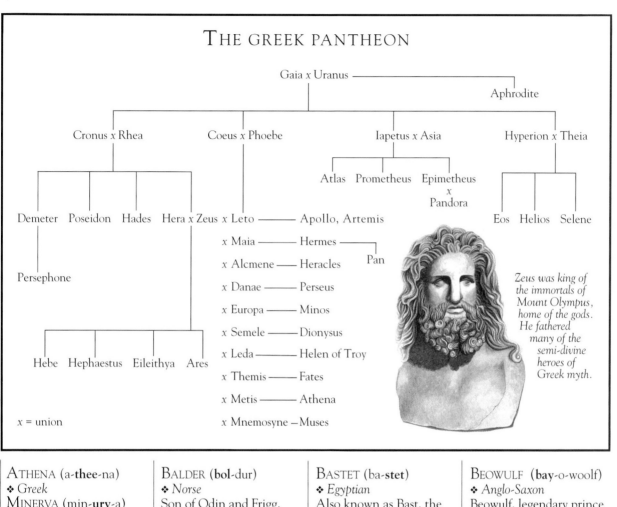

Gaia *x* Uranus

Aphrodite

Cronus *x* Rhea — Coeus *x* Phoebe — Iapetus *x* Asia — Hyperion *x* Theia

Atlas Prometheus Epimetheus
x
Pandora

Demeter Poseidon Hades Hera *x* Zeus *x* Leto ——— Apollo, Artemis

Eos Helios Selene

Persephone

x Maia ——— Hermes
x Alcmene —— Heracles   Pan
x Danae ——— Perseus
x Europa ——— Minos
x Semele ——— Dionysus
x Leda ——— Helen of Troy
x Themis ——— Fates
x Metis ——— Athena
x Mnemosyne — Muses

Hebe Hephaestus Eileithya Ares

x = union

Zeus was king of the immortals of Mount Olympus, home of the gods. He fathered many of the semi-divine heroes of Greek myth.

ATHENA (a-thee-na)
❖ *Greek*
MINERVA (min-urv-a)
❖ *Roman*
The goddess of wisdom and the daughter of Zeus and the wise Titaness Metis (whom Zeus turned into a fly and swallowed), Athena helped many heroes, including Heracles, Perseus, and Bellerophon. On her shield she had the head of Medusa, which turned her enemies to stone. Athens was named after her.

ARURU (ah-roor-roo)
❖ *Sumerian*
Aruru is the goddess of creation. She created Enkidu out of clay to be the friend and rival of the hero Gilgamesh.

BALDER (bol-dur)
❖ *Norse*
Son of Odin and Frigg, the wise and beautiful Balder was the most beloved of the gods. All things, save a sprig of mistletoe, swore not to hurt him. Through Loki's malice, Balder was slain with this mistletoe by his blind brother, Hoder. After the final battle of Ragnarok, Balder will return to lead mankind.

BAMAPAMA (ba-ma-pa-ma)
❖ *Australian Aboriginal*
Bamapama is a "crazy man", a trickster who breaks taboos and delights in stirring up arguments. Another name for him is Ure.

BASTET (ba-stet)
❖ *Egyptian*
Also known as Bast, the Egyptian cat goddess Bastet is a daughter of Re, the sun god. In her fiercer aspect she is depicted as a lioness named Sekhmet, however she is also the goddess of love and fertility. The centre of her worship was the city of Bubastis.

BENTEN (ben-tun)
❖ *Japanese*
The Shinto goddess of beauty, wealth, and fertility, Benten is also associated with the arts and with educational success. She married a serpent king and is often represented riding upon a serpent or a dragon.

BEOWULF (bay-o-woolf)
❖ *Anglo-Saxon*
Beowulf, legendary prince of the Geats (a tribe that lived in what is now southern Sweden), is the hero of an 8th-century epic poem. Beowulf travels to Heorot, the hall of King Hrothgar, and slays first the monster Grendel, and then Grendel's even fiercer mother.

BRAN (bran)
❖ *Celtic*
Bran, son of Febal, is the hero of an Irish epic in which he and his men travel from one magic island to another. When they return home, so much time has passed that they are only remembered as a legend.

CADMUS (cad-mus)
❖ *Greek*
Cadmus was the brother of Europa, who was carried off by Zeus. While searching for his sister, Cadmus was sent by the god Apollo to found the city of Thebes. When Cadmus asked for followers to people the city, Athena gave him some serpent's teeth to sow in the ground. A tough warrior race sprang up from the earth and became the first citizens of Thebes.

CHARON (ka-ron)
❖ *Greek*
One of the gods in Hades, the Underworld, grey-bearded Charon ferries the souls of the dead across the River Styx in return for a small coin.

Demeter, goddess of corn

CHIMAERA (kim-ear-a)
❖ *Greek*
A fire-breathing monster with the head of a lion, body of a goat, and tail of a serpent, the Chimaera ravaged the realm of King Iobates until the hero Bellerophon slew it.

CHUKU (choo-koo)
❖ *West African, Ashanti*
Chuku is the supreme god of the Ibo of southeastern Nigeria and the father of the earth goddess Ale.

COYOTE (ky-oh-tee)
❖ *Native American*
Mischievous, cunning, and endlessly resourceful, the trickster Coyote (sometimes called Hare) is both a comic and shocking figure in Native American mythology. Whether behaving well or badly, he seems to represent a kind of essential appetite for life.

CUCHULAIN (koo-kul-in)
❖ *Irish*
Cuchulain is the hero of the Ulster Cycle of Irish stories, which are full of fighting and bloodshed. He was known as the Hound of Ulster because he accidentally killed the watchdog belonging to Culann, a blacksmith, and as penance had to take the dog's place for a time. When fighting, Cuchulain was terrifying: one eye bulged and the other shrank into his head; his mouth gaped, his hair bristled and a column of dark blood rose up from his head.

DAEDALUS (deed-a-lus)
❖ *Greek*
Daedalus was a famous craftsman and inventor from Athens. After murdering his nephew, Talos, he served King Minos of Crete and devised the maze in which the Minotaur was kept. With his son, Icarus, he tried to escape from Crete using wings made of feathers and wax. But Icarus flew too near the sun, the wax binding his wings melted, and he fell to his death.

DEMETER (de-mee-ter)
❖ *Greek*
CERES (seer-eez)
❖ *Roman*
Demeter is the corn goddess and the mother of Persephone. When Persephone was snatched away by Hades, god of the Underworld, Demeter's grief made the world barren. So Zeus arranged for Persephone to return to Demeter for six months of every year.

DEVI (deh-vee)
❖ *Indian*
Devi, the Hindu great mother goddess, also appears under many other names, including Parvati (wife of Shiva and mother of Ganesha, the elephant-headed god), Durga, and the bloodthirsty Kali.

DIONYSUS (die-on-eye-sus)
❖ *Greek*
BACCHUS (back-us)
❖ *Roman*
The god of wine and ecstasy, Dionysus is the son of Zeus and a mortal woman, Semele. She insisted that Zeus appear to her undisguised and was immediately struck dead by the lightning that flashed from his glorious presence. Zeus rescued her unborn child. Dionysus loved wild parties with his women followers, the Maenads, and his male followers, the Satyrs.

EA (ay-ah)
❖ *Sumerian*
The god of earth, water, and wisdom, Ea sent the Seven Sages to teach skills to mankind. He is the father of Adapa, the earth's first man.

EARTH-MAKER
❖ *Native American*
Earth-maker is the benevolent supreme god of the Maidu of California; his rival is the trickster Coyote.

ENKIDU (en-kee-doo)
❖ *Sumerian*
The friend and rival of Gilgamesh, Enkidu was a Sumerian/Akkadian hero.

ENLIL (en-lil)
❖ *Sumerian*
Enlil, the air god, separated the heavens from the earth.

ERLIK (airr-leek)
❖ *Siberian*
This evil spirit was made from mud by Ulgan, the creator, to be his helper. Erlik became the lord of the dead.

EROS (ear-oss)
❖ *Greek*
Cupid (kew-pid)
❖ *Roman*
The god of love and son of Aphrodite, Eros is a beautiful boy. He has a quiver full of arrows, which he shoots at people to make them fall in love.

ESTSANATLEHI (est-sa-nat-le-hee)
❖ *Native American*
Estsánatlehi means "the changing woman", for she grows old during the winter, but becomes young again in spring.

FENRIS-WOLF (fen-ris wolf)
❖ *Norse*
The ferocious Fenris-wolf was tied up with a magic chain, Gleipnir, by Tyr, the god of war. It will break free at Ragnorok.

FIRST CREATOR
❖ *Native American*
First Creator, together with Lone Man, creates the world in the creation myth of the Mandan Sioux. First Creator is said to have turned into a coyote when his work was finished.

FREYJA (**fray**-ya)
❖ *Norse*
Freyja, the goddess of love, fertility, and of seeresses is the most beautiful of the gods. Her most precious possession is the necklace Brisingamen, which she won from the dwarfs. She can turn herself into a falcon and often travels in a carriage drawn by two cats.

FREYR (**frayr**)
❖ *Norse*
God of fertility and plenty and the brother of Freyja, Freyr owned a magic ship, Skidbladnir, that could hold all the gods, yet could be folded up small when not in use. He fell in love with Gerd, a giant's daughter. Wooing her cost him his sword, which will leave him weaponless at the battle of Ragnarok.

FRIGG (**frig**)
❖ *Norse*
Frigg is the goddess of childbirth and the wife of Odin. Like him, she can see into the future.

GANESHA (ga-**nay**-sha)
❖ *Indian*
Ganesha is the elephant-headed son of Shiva and Parvati and the Hindu god of good fortune. Those beginning any new enterprise pray to him.

Freyja, goddess of love

GEB (**gebb**)
❖ *Egyptian*
The earth god Geb married the sky goddess Nut, and is the father of Isis and Osiris.

GHEDE (ga-**hed**-a)
❖ *Haitian*
The top-hatted god of death in Voodoo mythology, Ghede is also known as Baron Samedi. He bestrides life and death and possesses all the knowledge of everyone who has died.

GIANTS, THE
❖ *Norse*
The frost giants are all descended from Ymir, the first frost giant, whom Odin slew. They are the brutal, devious, and envious enemies of the gods, and will fight against them at Ragnarok.

GILGAMESH (**gil**-ga-mesh)
❖ *Sumerian*
The epic of Gilgamesh was developed by the Akkadian peoples of Babylon and Assyria from the myths of the Sumerians. Gilgamesh was a semi-divine hero-king of the city of Uruk, who searched for the secret of immortality.

GLOOSKAP (**gloo**-skap)
❖ *Native American*
The major hero of the Algonquin tribes, Glooskap brought many gifts to men and defeated various enemies before sailing away in his canoe.

GORGONS, THE (**gore**-gonz)
❖ *Greek*
The Gorgons lived in the far west and had snakes for hair, bodies covered in scales, tusks, and stares so horrifying that they turned people to stone. They were sisters, and their names were Stheno, Euryale, and Medusa. When the hero Perseus killed Medusa, the winged horse Pegasus sprang from her headless body.

HADES (**hay**-deez)
❖ *Greek*
DIS (**deess**)
❖ *Roman*
Hades is the god of the Underworld and the brother of Zeus. His wife is Persephone. His realm, which is also named Hades, lies on the other side of the River Styx. Hades contains Tartarus, where the wicked are punished, and the beautiful Elysian Fields, where the virtuous enjoy their reward.

HEIMDALL (**haym**-dahl)
❖ *Norse*
Heimdall is the watchman of Asgard and the guardian of the rainbow bridge Bifrost. His eyesight and hearing are very acute. Heimdall will blow the horn Gjall to signal Ragnarok, the last battle between gods and giants.

HEPHAESTUS (heff-**eest**-uss)
❖ *Greek*
VULCAN (**vul**-can)
❖ *Roman*
The god of the forge, Hephaestus is the husband of Aphrodite. His parents, Zeus and Hera, quarrelled, and Zeus flung him from Olympus, leaving him lame in one leg.

HERA (**hair**-a)
❖ *Greek*
JUNO (**joo**-noh)
❖ *Roman*
The haughty wife of Zeus, Hera is a goddess of marriage and childbirth. There are many stories of her anger at Zeus's amorous escapades.

Heimdall, the watchman

HERACLES (**hair**-a-kleez)
❖ *Greek*
HERCULES (**her**-kyoo-leez)
❖ *Roman*
Heracles was the greatest of all the Greek heroes, and is especially famous for the twelve Labours he undertook. Zeus was his father, and a mortal, Alcmene, his mother. Hera, Zeus's jealous wife, was thus his deadly enemy and placed many obstacles in his path.

HERMES (**her**-meez)
❖ *Greek*
MERCURY (**mer**-kyoo-ree)
❖ *Roman*
The son of Zeus and the nymph Maia, Hermes is the messenger of the gods. He wears winged sandals and sometimes a *petarsus*, a hat worn by Greek travellers. Hermes is also the patron god of merchants and thieves. He escorts the souls of the dead to Hades.

HORUS (**hore**-us)
❖ *Egyptian*
Horus, the falcon-headed sky god, is the dutiful son of Isis and Osiris. Horus is the sworn enemy of Set, who murdered Osiris. Horus and Set are locked in eternal struggle.

ILMARINEN (**eel**-ma-ren-en)
❖ *Finnish*
The smith of the heavens, Ilmarinen forged the magical mill of plenty called the Sampo.

Hermes, messenger of the gods

ISHTAR (**ish**-tar)
❖ *Sumerian*
Also called Inanna, Ishtar is the goddess of love and war. She became furious when Gilgamesh rejected her love and asked the god Anu to create the Bull of Heaven to ravage Gilgamesh's kingdom.

Horus, the sky god

ISIS (**eye**-sis)
❖ *Egyptian*
The Egyptian mother goddess, Isis is the daughter of Nut and Geb. She is the sister and wife of Osiris and the mother of Horus, the falcon-headed sky god.

IZANAGI (iz-an-**nah**-gee)
❖ *Japanese*
In Shinto mythology, Izanagi created the Japanese islands, together with his wife, Izanami. After she became goddess of the Underworld, Izanagi created several other gods. These included Amaterasu, the goddess of the sun, Tsuki-Yomi, the god of the moon, and Susanowo, the god of the tempest.

IZANAMI (iz-an-**nah**-mee)
❖ *Japanese*
The female spouse and opposite of Izanagi, Izanami died giving birth to Fire, and then became the goddess of the Underworld.

KAMRUSEPAS (kam-**roos**-pas)
❖ *Hittite*
The Hittite goddess of spells and healing.

KAMUI (**ka**-moo-wee)
❖ *Japan, Ainu*
Kamui is the sky god of the Ainu, an aboriginal people living on the northern Japanese island of Hokkaido. He is also called Tuntu, support, or pillar, of the world.

KUMUSH (kum-**ush**)
❖ *Native American*
Kumush, "the Old Man of the Ancients", is the central figure in the creation myth of the Modoc of northern California. He created the Native American people by fetching bones from the underworld land of the spirits before leaving this world for ever for a home in the sky.

KUNITOKOTATTCHI (**kun**-i-tok-**oh**-ta-chee)
❖ *Japanese*
The remote supreme deity of Shinto belief, who grew as a reed in the primeval swamp. His name means "eternal land ruler", and he is believed to live on the slopes of sacred Mount Fuji, whose spirit, Fujiyama, is the guardian of the nation.

KURENT (kur-**rent**)
❖ *Serbian*
The stories about the sly trickster god Kurent, who makes a fool out of mankind's representative, the giant Kranyatz, by getting him drunk with wine, were collected in Carniola in Serbia. The tales record a native, pagan, Slavonic mythology, to which Christian elements – in particular a single, all-knowing god – have been added.

KWAKU-ANANSE (**kwa**-koo-a-**nan**-say)
❖ *West African, Ashanti*
The spider-man trickster of West Africa. Kwaku-Ananse's exploits lie behind many of the Brer Rabbit fables of African Americans, made famous in the Uncle Remus stories of J. C. Harris.

LEMMINKAINEN (lem-**mink**-eye-non)
❖ *Finnish*
Lemminkainen helps Vainamoinen and Ilmarinen steal the magic mill of plenty, the Sampo, from Louhi, the witch of the Northlands.

Ishtar, goddess of love and war

LOKI (**lo**-kee)
❖ *Norse*
The trickster Loki is the son of two giants, Farbauti and Laufey, and is Odin's foster brother. Loki's playfulness often caused harm to the gods and, in the end, his tricks led to the death of Balder. Imprisoned by the gods for this crime, Loki will break free to lead the giants against the gods at the battle of Ragnarok. Loki's children include the Fenris-wolf, the Midgard serpent, Hel, and Sleipnir, Odin's eight-legged steed.

LOUHI (**loo**-hee)
❖ *Finnish*
Louhi the witch is the mistress of the North and the enemy of the heroes of the *Kalevala*.

Maui-of-a-Thousand-Tricks

MAUI (**mah**-oo-ee)
❖ *Polynesian*
Maui fished up the islands of the South Pacific from the ocean bed, stole fire for human beings, and had many other adventures. He is known as "Maui-of-a-Thousand-Tricks".

MERLIN (**mer**-lin)
❖ *Celtic*
Merlin was the wizard and seer who helped to bring up and advise King Arthur. He later fell in love with a scheming fairy named Nimue. He taught Nimue magic, and she cruelly repaid him by imprisoning him for ever in an enchanted wood.

MINOTAUR, THE (**my**-no-tore)
❖ *Greek*
The monstrous offspring of Pasiphae, the wife of King Minos of Crete, the flesh-eating Minotaur was half man, half bull. It lived in a labyrinth devised by the craftsman Daedalus and was fed on human flesh – until the hero Theseus killed it.

MICTLANTECUHTLI (mek-**tlahn**-ha-coot-lee)
❖ *Aztec*
This god of the dead rules the silent, peaceful kingdom of Mictlan.

MIDGARD SERPENT, THE (**mid**-gard **ser**-pent)
❖ *Norse*
One of Loki's and the giantess Angrboda's monstrous children, this menacing sea serpent (also known as Jormungand) encircles the world of human beings. At Ragnarok, it will be killed by Thor, who will die from its poisonous bite.

MORRIGAN (**morr**-i-gun)
❖ *Irish*
This goddess of war appears on battlefields in the shape of a crow. She fell in love with the hero Cuchulain. When he rejected her, she became his bitter enemy.

NANA-BULUKU (**na**-na-ba-**loo**-koo)
❖ *West African, Fon*
The creator god of the Fon of Bénin, Nana-Buluku is the father and mother of Mawu and Lisa, who shaped the world that Nana-Buluku had created. Mawu is associated with the moon and with fertility; Lisa with the sun and with war. Mawu and Lisa's children are the Vodu, the lesser gods.

NORNS, THE (nornz)
❖ *Norse*
The Norns – Fate, Being, and Necessity – are the three maidens who guard the spring of fate at one of the roots of Yggdrasil, the world tree.

NUT (**noot**)
❖ *Egyptian*
Nut, the sky goddess is the wife of Geb and the mother of Isis and Osiris.

NYANKONPON (ny-**ang**-cong-pon)
❖ *West African, Ashanti*
Nyankonpon is the sky god whose tales are won by Kwaku-Ananse.

ODIN (**oh**-din)
❖ *Norse*
The oldest and the highest of the gods, Odin is the god of battle. He gave one of his eyes to drink from the spring of Mimir, which brought wisdom. He won the mead of poetry from the giants, and it is his gift to men.

Odin, god of battle

ORPHEUS (**or**-fee-uss)
❖ *Greek*
Son of Apollo and the muse Calliope, Orpheus was the greatest musician ever. He pursued his wife, Eurydice, into the Underworld to persuade Hades to let her return to life. But Orpheus lost her when he looked back to see if she was following.

OSIRIS (o-**sire**-is)
❖ *Egyptian*
Osiris, husband of Isis, was a fertility god who taught people farming. He was murdered by his brother, Set, and became judge of the dead.

PAN (**pan**)
❖ *Greek*
FAUNUS (**fawn**-us)
❖ *Roman*
The son of Hermes, Pan is the god of wild places and of shepherds and their flocks. He has the horns and legs of a goat. Pan plays haunting music on a set of reed pipes called a Syrinx. He can inspire fear – "panic" – in people and animals.

P'AN-KU (pahn-**koo**)
❖ *Chinese*
The gigantic being who burst out of the cosmic egg, P'an-ku created the world and everything in it.

PERSEPHONE (per-**seff**-on-nee)
❖ *Greek*
PROSERPINA (pro-**sir**-pi-na)
❖ *Roman*
The beautiful daughter of Demeter, Persephone was snatched away by Hades, who made her his queen in the Underworld.

PERSEUS (**per**-see-us)
❖ *Greek*
Perseus, one of the best known Greek heroes, was the son of Zeus and a mortal woman, Danae. With the help of the goddess Athena and the god Hermes, he slew the Gorgon Medusa and saved Andromeda, his future wife, from a sea monster.

POSEIDON (poss-**eye**-don)
❖ *Greek*
NEPTUNE (**nep**-tune)
❖ *Roman*
Poseidon is the god of the sea and the brother of Zeus and Hades.

PROMETHEUS (prom-**ee**-thee-us)
❖ *Greek*
The only Titan to fight with Zeus against Cronus, Prometheus angered Zeus by giving fire to humans. He was cruelly punished until Heracles freed him.

QUETZALCOATL (**ket**-sahl-koh-**ah**-tuhl)
❖ *Aztec*
Quetzalcoatl is the divine priest who struggles with his warrior brother, Tezcatlipoca. With his twin, Xolotl, he made people by grinding up the bones of the ancient dead and sprinkling them with his own blood.

Poseidon, god of the sea

RE (**ray**)
❖ *Egyptian*
Re, or Ra, the sun god, is, as Atum, the creator god of ancient Egypt. Every night Re does battle with the gigantic serpent of chaos named Apep. One story about Re relates how, in his old age, he was tricked into revealing his secret name by Isis. The knowledge made her immortal.

Re, the sun god

SAOSHYANT (**sow**-shyunt)
❖ *Iranian*
The saviour in the Zoroastrian religion, Saoshyant will come at the end of the world to scour away all traces of the evil Ahriman and bring into being a new, perfect world. The dead will rise and a mighty stream of molten metal will pour from the earth. This will be like warm milk to the good, but the bad will suffer agonies as their sins are burned away.

SEDNA (**sed**-nuh)
❖ *Inuit*
Sedna is the mother of the sea beasts and queen of the underworld, Adlivun. She is the most important figure in Inuit mythology, for by releasing or withholding the fish and animals that the Inuit people hunt, she grants life or death.

SET (**set**)
❖ *Egyptian*
Set, also known as Seth, is lord of the desert and god of storms, confusion, and destruction. Set murdered his own brother, Osiris, by sealing him in a coffin. His eternal enemy is Horus, the sky god, the son of Isis and Osiris.

SHIVA (**shee**-vah)
❖ *Indian*
Shiva is the great destroyer, but in this way he creates the conditions for new life to flourish. He forms part of the "trimurti," a trinity of Hindu gods that includes Vishnu, the helper of mankind, and Brahma, the creator. Shiva's wife is called Parvati, one of the forms of the goddess Devi. Shiva rides on Nandi, a white bull who is the guardian of animals.

Quetzalcoatl, the divine priest

SUSANOWO (soo-sa-**no**-woah)
❖ *Japan*
The spiteful storm god of Shinto belief, Susanowo's destructive actions brought his sensitive sister Amaterasu, the sun goddess, near to despair.

TALIESIN (**tal**-i-ay-sin)
❖ *Welsh*
The legendary Welsh bard Taliesin was originally a humble boy named Gwion. By accident, a magic potion brewed by the witch Ceridwen gave him amazing knowledge of the past, the present, and the future.

Shiva, the great destroyer

TELEPINU (tell-uh-**pee**-noo)
❖ *Hittite*
The god of agriculture and the son of the weather and fertility god, Telepinu nearly laid waste to the earth in his anger. The goddess Kamrusepas finally succeeded in calming him down with her magic, and fertility returned to the earth once more.

TEZCATLIPOCA (tes-**kaht**-lee-**poh**-ka)
❖ *Aztec*
Tezcatlipoca, "the smoking mirror," is the Aztec warrior god and the god of vengeance. It is he whose cruel tricks and bitter jealousy prove the undoing of the pure and innocent Quetzalcoatl, the plumed serpent god.

THESEUS (**thee**-see-us)
❖ *Greek*
Theseus was the son of King Aegeus of Athens, or, in some versions, Poseidon, god of the sea. One of the best known of all the Greek heroes, the Athenian prince's most famous exploit was the slaying of the flesh-eating Minotaur. This he achieved with the help of Ariadne, the king of Crete's daughter.

THOR (thor)
❖ *Norse*

Son of Odin and the Earth, Thor is the sky and thunder god. He carries a hammer, Miollnir, which is his most precious possession; when he throws it, it always returns to his hand. Many Vikings wore hammer amulets in his honour. Thor had many battles with the giants, and once tried to fish up the Midgard serpent. His wife is golden-haired Sif, a fertility goddess.

TUATHA DE DANANN
(**thyoo**-a-ha day **dai-**nan)
❖ *Celtic*

The Irish gods, including Lugh, the sun god and the father of Cuchulain. Their chief was Dagda, god of life and death.

TYR (**ti**-uh)
❖ *Norse*

Tyr is the god of war. He sacrificed his left hand when binding of the Fenris-wolf with the magic fetter Gleipnir.

Miollnir, the hammer of Thor

ULGAN (**ool**-gun)
❖ *Siberian*

The high god of the Tartars, Ulgan created the world out of mud, which his helper, Erlik, fetched from the bottom of the ocean.

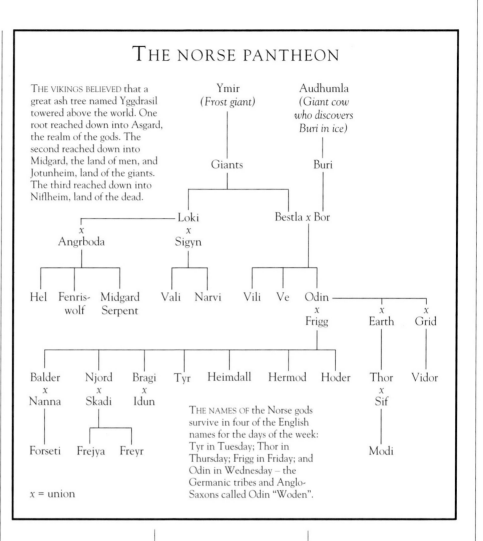

THE NORSE PANTHEON

THE VIKINGS BELIEVED that a great ash tree named Yggdrasil towered above the world. One root reached down into Asgard, the realm of the gods. The second reached down into Midgard, the land of men, and Jotunheim, land of the giants. The third reached down into Niflheim, land of the dead.

Ymir
(Frost giant)

Audhumla
(Giant cow who discovers Buri in ice)

Giants

Buri

Loki
x
Angrboda

x
Sigyn

Bestla *x* Bor

Hel · Fenris-wolf · Midgard Serpent

Vali · Narvi

Vili · Ve · Odin
x
Frigg

x
Earth

x
Grid

Balder
x
Nanna

Njord
x
Skadi

Bragi
x
Idun

Tyr · Heimdall · Hermod · Hoder

Thor
x
Sif

Vidor

Forseti · Frejya · Freyr

THE NAMES OF the Norse gods survive in four of the English names for the days of the week: Tyr in Tuesday; Thor in Thursday; Frigg in Friday; and Odin in Wednesday – the Germanic tribes and Anglo-Saxons called Odin "Woden".

Modi

x = union

URANUS (you-**rain**-us)
❖ *Greek*

Uranus was the god of the heavens. His children by Gaia, the earth goddess, were the race of Titans, including Cronus ("Time"), who killed him. Aphrodite, the goddess of love, sprang from the foam of the sea when Cronus cut him into pieces.

UTNAPISHTIM
(oot-na-**pish**-tim)
❖ *Sumerian*

Utnapishtim and his wife were the only survivors of the flood caused by the god Ea. Utnapishtim was Gilgamesh's ancestor.

UZUME (oo-**zoo**-mee)
❖ *Japanese*

Ama-no-uzume is the Japanese goddess associated with the dawn whose rude and uproarious dance enticed Amaterasu, the sun goddess, from the cave where she hid.

VALKYRIES, THE
(val-**ky**-reez)
❖ *Norse*

Daughters of Odin, the Valkyries are female warrior spirits who ride into battle, giving victory or defeat as Odin wills. They wait on the dead warriors in the halls of Valhalla.

ZEUS (**zyoos**)
❖ *Greek*
JUPITER (**jyoo**-pi-ter)
❖ *Roman*

The greatest of the gods, Zeus waged war against his father, Cronus, and the other Titans. He is married to Hera, but has had many love affairs.

Valhalla, Odin's hall for heroes

INDEX

Numbers in **bold** refer to an entry in Who's Who in Mythology.

Acknowledgements

Photographic Credits
t=top, b=bottom, c=centre, l=left, r=right

AKG London/Erich Lessing: 130tl.
American Museum of Natural History 53br, 75tr; Courtesy Department Library Services (neg. no. 14471) 37tr.
Ancient Art & Architecture Collection/Ronald Sheridan 30bl, 45br, 98tl, 109br, 147tr, 154tl, 177tr; B. Wilson front cover, 96tl.
Antikensammlungen und Glyptothek, Munich 104tl.
Ardea London 59tl.
Ashmolean Museum, Oxford 23b.
The Bridgeman Art Library/Bibliothèque Nationale 157tr; British Museum, London, front cover, 8, 140tl; Bernard Cox/Archaeological Museum 170tl.
The British Library (Add. 10,294 f.94) 158bl.
The British Museum 16l, 29tr, 46bl, back cover, 84bl, 80tl, 87br, 102, 103tr, 105tr, 110bl, 112tl, 145br, 149tr, 150tl, 151br, front cover, 168tl.
Bruce Coleman Ltd /Mr R. V. Bryant: 124b; Thomas Buchholz 20bl; Gerald Cubitt 43tr; Stephen J. Krasemann 74t; Hans Reinhard 72tl.
Michael Diggin 161tr.
C.M Dixon 94bl, 96bl, 119tl, 138bl, 175tr.
Ecoscene/Whitty 92tl.
Finnish Tourist Board 54br.
Michael & Patricia Fogden 142tl.
Werner Forman Archive /Arhus Kunst Museum, Denmark 165tr; National Museum of Ireland: 126b; Schindler Collection, New York: 36tl; Statens Historiska Museum, Stockholm, front cover, 18tl, front cover, 64tl;
Fortean Picture Library/Allen Kennedy 128bl.
Germanisches National Museum, Nürnberg 88tl.
Sonia Halliday Photographs 166cl.
Hamburgisches Museum für Völkerkunde 68l.
Robert Harding Picture Library 42bl, 108tl, 113tr, 146bl, 157br; Michael Jenner back cover, 127tr; Robert McLeod 25tr.

Michael Holford 38tl, 45tr, 48tl, 60tl, 61tr, 81tr, 84tl, 99tr, 107br, 144l, 146tl, 174tl.
Neil Holmes 88bl, 107tr.
The Hutchison Library 42tl, 31tr, 77r, 117tr, 177br.
Instituto Nacional de Antropologia e Historia, Mexico 141cr.
Japan National Tourist Organization 26tl.
La Belle Aurore/Steve Davey & Juliet Coombe 29br.
Collection Musée de l'Homme, Paris 76tl.
National Museum of Denmark, Copenhagen 63cr, 120tl, 122cl, 164cl.
National Museum of Ireland front cover, 90bl.
National Museum of Scotland 159tr.
NHPA/Orion Press 24tl.
Oslo Ship Museum 65tl, 118bl.
OSF /Animals Animals/Roger Brown 28tl; Richard Kolar 35tr; Martin Chillmaid 19tr; Jeff Foott 152-153; Breck P. Kent 33tr; John Netherton 100-101; Ben Osborne 51tr.
Planet Earth Pictures/David Redfern: 66bl.
Pitt Rivers Museum, Oxford 56bl, 69tr, 169tr.
Poseidon Pictures/Peter J. Terry: 138tl.
Rijksmuseum voor Volkenkunde, Leiden/Ben Grishaauer 93tr.
© photo **RMN** 44tl, 52tl, 154bl.
Royal Geographical Society/Paul Harris 34tl.
Matti Ruotsalainen 56tl.
Scala 148tl.
Harry Smith Collection/Polunin Collection 131tr.
Statens Historiska Museum, Stockholm 62tl, 162bl.
Turkish Tourist Office 170bl.
University Museum of Archaeology and Anthropology, Cambridge back cover, 127br.
Universitäts und Landesbibliothek, Bonn 89tr.
Jerry Young 14-15, 22tl, 40-41, 78-79, 136-137, 178-179.
Wales Tourist Board 114tl, 115br.
Michel Zabé 143tr.
Zefa Pictures/Konrad Helbig 95cr.

Dorling Kindersley would like to thank:
Mr G. Bates; the Corbally Stourton Art Gallery, London; Sheila Dignen; Felicity Devlin of the National Museum of Ireland; Lucy Godman; Jim Hamill of the Museum of Mankind, London; Mr Hamim of the Indonesian Embassy, London; Robin Hunter; The Keeper's Secretary, Pre-history and Romano-British Dept, the British Museum, London; Kew Gardens; Barbara Ann Kipfer, Ph. D.; Father M. Kostic; Dr Kuniholm of the Malcolm & Carolyn Einer Laboratory for Aegean and Near Eastern Archaeology, New York; Meg McCulloch of the Australian Tourist Commission, London; and Erja Tikka of the Finnish Embassy, London, for their help in producing this book.

Illustrations pp. 180-187: Fiona Bell Currie

Index: Lynn Bresler